Aussie Jour

Aussie Journeyman by Alvin Gardiner
Published by Australian Ebook Publisher
© Alvin Gardiner

1st Edition 2017, pbk.
ISBN: 9780987611604
Designer: Julia Lefik, Australian eBook Publisher

Aussie
Journeyman

Memoir of a Touring Tennis Professional

Alvin Gardiner

Aussie
Journeyman

Australian
eBook
Publisher

Alvin Gardiner

Chapter 1

Getting Started

It was near midnight when we cruised into Irún, a small border control town that sits between France and Spain. The two Spanish guards in their little hut were getting a bit ticked off with the two dishevelled looking Aussies who were demanding entry into the country. One guard was unshaven and obviously more than a bit inebriated. We saw a couple of wine bottles on the floor of the guard hut. He suddenly snapped. Both guards had been repeatedly yelling to us, "Francia, Francia !" In other words, "Get your butts outta here and go back to France". Finally the drunker one reached down to his holster, pulled out a pistol, cocked it and put it to my temple and said "Francia?" This time, more emphatically. Obviously the guard had undergone charisma bypass surgery. I turned to my buddy, Wayne, who also received the pistol treatment, and said, "You know, I think he has a good point, we probably should head back to France".

No one was shot that night in Irún but we were scared shitless. We ended up high-tailing it out of there with our other two tennis compadres. In the early hours of the morning we eventually found a way into the dreaded Spain through the back door of the Pyrénées Mountains, possibly via Andorra. We are still not sure of the route.

Seems like bad things always happened when I went to Spain. It was just a bump in the road, the endless road of the touring Aussie tennis player. Spain during the Franco regime was a dark place, not the friendliest place for foreigners and not the place to get into any trouble. Trouble seemed to follow us there in those times.

I'm not sure what you would call us in those days. We would like to be known as tennis pros but we were hardly making any money as professionals. Perhaps tennis bums would be a more appropriate term. We were on the road for six to seven months a year, away from Australia and travelling between towns or countries every week. One week it would be train travel, the next week car, sometimes plane and occasionally hitching a ride. It was not all glamour and glitz. Well, hardly any glamour, very little glitz. There were tough days. With no money coming in, battling constant injuries and consequently not winning too many matches, it made for interesting yet trying times. But we were following our dreams, striving for the heights that a lot of our heroes, the Aussie champions, had reached. A tough journey but we loved it. Some ups and downs. But this particular trip into Spain was a downer and the ensuing few weeks were worse. This was the early 1970s.

Tennis turned Open in 1968. This meant there was no distinction between professionals and amateurs anymore. Everyone was the same breed. Prior to 1968, tennis players did not get any prize money, just a nice trophy, some tennis gear and a title or two. These so called amateurs had to negotiate a deal with a tournament director in the form of expenses or in other words a guarantee of money to appear at their tournament. The "shamateurs" received bigger guarantees if their rankings or international status was impressive. There was one band of professionals, though, formed by the great Jack Kramer, who was champion of the world in his day and later turned a visionary entrepreneur. He got together the best amateurs, guaranteed them a handsome salary for a year or two then hit the road with his troupe.

These guys did one-night stands and played each other hundreds of times from California to Calcutta. There were some tremendous head to head rivalries especially between the best

6

player Pancho Gonzales, "Gorgo" (the big cheese) and the incoming newcomer, usually the best amateur champion who was eventually signed pro by Jack. Some of the rivalries were Gonzales v Rosewall, Gonzales v Laver, Gonzales v Hoad but "Gorgo" was the undisputed king for a long time. Australia's Lew Hoad was introduced as the next best contender for the crown of World Champion.

These professionals could not compete in the major championships, the Grand Slam events or represent their country in Davis Cup. Once they signed that contract they were done with winning titles and trophies. But they were making some money to feed their families. Imagine how many majors Gonzales could have won if he wasn't in exile? Maybe he could be pushing Sampras and Federer for most Slams won. But the ageless Gonzales was back at Wimbledon and Forest titles for those first professional Opens of 1968.

How did those amateurs survive? Well, sometimes they were referred to as shamateurs because they did get a few shekels under the table. They were like semi-professionals. The International Lawn Tennis Association condoned all this. You were allowed to receive expenses and/or appearance money to play a tournament. The players had to sell themselves to a tournament but the extent of their fee was usually dependant on their ranking, either national or world ranking. Of course, the four Grand Slams had all the players for zero down. The players wanted to do well in the majors to increase their status on the world stage. The Slam organisers must have been laughing, no prize money to shell out, they just raked in the money from the TV rights and the big attendances at the gate.

Naturally these amateurs would play in all tournaments and were eligible to represent their country in Davis Cup. Eventually the world's best could sell out to Kramer for a handsome salary guarantee and turn their back on the shamateur days.

So it was a bit of a parody really. Everyone was getting money in some form. It was ludicrous that the very best players were banned from the main showcase events. And there was little doubt that Kramer's men were the best players on the planet. Nowadays, everyone is a professional. The one exception is the American collegiate player who must remain amateur to keep a scholarship status. But even the college players have ways around that if they win some money in a tournament outside college competition, that is legitimate expenses in lieu of prize money.

So this was the scenario when I first hit the road in 1969. My journey had just started. Open Tennis was still a baby, only one year old. Technically in order to travel overseas and try our own hand as a professional tennis player we had to obtain permission from the Lawn Tennis Association of Australia (LTAA). Permission to go to work? It seemed a bit crazy. We were referred to as registered players and had to get our letter, our exit visa if you will, before taking off to tour the world. Were we copying our communist friends in Europe with their similar policies on outside travel?

Looking back, in early 1969 I was a naïve 18 year old eager to go play. I think that the LTAA wanted some hold over their players so they had some left to play Davis Cup for Australia. What if everyone took off to win some of this new prize money and nobody stayed for the pure white Davis Cup? Prize money would not arrive at Davis Cup level until years later when corporate sponsors like NEC became involved. So they were still playing for a trophy albeit a big assed trophy, that wonderful perpetual trophy, The Davis Cup.

I think that Australia did not want a repeat of the brouhaha in the early 1960s when some of the Aussie great players were ostracized for not making themselves available for Davis Cup. They saw a great opportunity to make some bread as appearance money on the elite Caribbean circuit. The top amateurs were paid well to play for a few weeks early in the season at the exotic resorts of the Caribbean.

I'm not familiar with the dirty details but three of the great Aussie stars, Ken Fletcher, Bob Hewitt, and Marty Mulligan were branded rebels for defying the LTAA and going to work in the Caribbean. Somehow the two superstars of Australian Tennis in the early 1960s now that Rod Laver had signed with Kramer, Roy Emerson and Fred Stolle, survived the rebel tag and were exonerated for their sins and they were kept as the backbone of the Davis Cup team. A lot of politics formed the LTAA. Subsequently the three rebels turned their backs on Australia: "Mull" (who was number two in the world) emigrated to Italy where his forebears came from, "Fletch" lived in Hong Kong to wheel and deal a million deals, and "Baldy" Bob Hewitt settled in South Africa. It appeared to be a brutal result for those three guys. The tennis establishment was brutal in those days.

I had no clue how to organise an overseas tennis tour. For me, this was my first time travelling overseas and I was young and green. Where do you go? Outer Mongolia? BFE? (Bloody F..ing Egypt, for the uninformed) or straight to Wimbledon? How do you enter tournaments or get there? There were a million questions to ask. Unfortunately we had no guidance, no one to advise us and show us the way. One of the grizzled Aussie veterans said to me "Son get yourself a bloody round-the-world air ticket and write to the ITF (International Tennis Federation) in Paris for a calendar of all the tennis events". OK, thanks mate, too easy. From that calendar, you had to write an individual letter to each tournament and request an invitation. Was the number two ranked junior in Australia worth $US100 and full hospitality for the week? I learned that would be a nice deal in 1969. Full hospitality meant free hotel and meals, and 100 of the beautiful greenbacks or it could be the equivalent in Italian lira or Spanish pesetas. But US dollars was the currency spoken. I felt a little like a whore writing to the tournament director and selling myself, telling him how great I was, as if they cared. What I needed was an agent. I never learned how the big stars did their negotiations although a lot of the deals were done in the tearoom at the All England Club Wimbledon during the Championships. The Wimbledon champion might demand $1000 to show up in, say, Istanbul or Teheran plus hospitality, of course. A little like the rock stars of today—we want a gazillion dollars, a Rolls Royce at our disposal, caviar every meal, a ton of cocaine, and wall-to-wall girls.

Mainly the tournaments we communicated with were the European ones. There were literally hundreds of tournaments all over the European continent from May to September. Do I play in France, Italy, Spain, Germany, or Holland? There were endless possibilities. And then there were the tournaments in Great Britain leading up to the big "W" and afterwards. They were often cash poor but sometimes they offered some private housing, which helped our pockets.

Apart from these guarantees, prize money was starting to grow now the professional doors were open. Gee, the winner of Wimbledon was getting a whopping £2,000 back in those new years of open tennis. Nowadays the winner receives two million dollars (men and women alike). As I said, my journey started in March 1969. I had my around-the-world air ticket thanks to my only sponsor, my parents. First stop, the South African Open in Johannesburg, followed by the Natal Open in Durban, South Africa. No idea why I went to Johannesburg first off. Guess some other Aussies were heading that way. It was still a tad early in the European season—might be some snow on the ground still—so the seasoned pros would work their way to the European courts with some random stops in Manila, perhaps, or in the middle east (Cairo, Tel Aviv, Saudi Arabia) or even Moscow (so sorry, we are Communist, no dollars for you, just a few roubles per diem). It helped to possess a good address book and later on get to talk to these envoys in that powerful Wimbledon tearoom. Make your deal over strawberries and cream six months ahead. But then again, it really sucked if you were a shit-kicker. Who would want you, a relative unknown?

My travel buddy was a nice guy from Perth, Tony Hammond. Tony's nickname was "Digger" for reasons unknown. He was from a well–to-do family in Perth and was the best junior player out of Western Australia. "Digger" was a very conservative kid, truly genuine, but as dry as a wooden gate. We wandering Aussie tennis guys seemed to travel in pairs. I teamed up with "Digger" because my regular partner, Ross Case, was planning to travel overseas the following year, 1970. We would team up then on the road that next year.

There was a comradeship amongst the Aussie players, maybe because we were a long way from home for a long time—some guys stayed away two years at a time to save money. Everyone tended to give support to his fellow mates. Perhaps this stemmed from the two World Wars when the Aussies fought in Gallipoli, in the trenches of Europe or North Africa. Maybe Tony received his name from the "Diggers", the term used for trench digging soldiers. Or maybe because his forehand was so ugly, like he was digging a trench with a shovel. It was funny, nearly all the Australian players had nicknames. Mine was Aggro—my initials are "A.G.". That was part of it, but truthfully it was because I did things the arduous way, no easy street for me, everything was aggravation, the hard way. Off I went on a training run, for example, I would love to do it in extreme weather, 110°F or snowing. No easy way. Let's go through some "aggro ", make it a challenge. I would love to climb Everest (even though I' m very scared of heights). Imagine the aggro involved. Life was not meant to be plain sailing. Plus, I think the nickname was a badge of respect. A few of the guys without nicknames were bits of dickheads. They had not earned a good moniker. Some of the named ones were: the "Snake" (my partner, Ross Case), "Flash" (Cliff Letcher), "Eddo" (Mark Edmonson), and "the Rookie" (Brad Drewett). There was also "Side Agate" (Syd Ball), Allan "Rolling" Stone, "Gobbles" (Geoff Masters), "Hessian" (Ray Ruffels) and the more mundane-named "J.A." (John Alexander), "Philby" (Phil Dent) and "Rochie" (Tony Roche). Also, there were the famous ones: "Rocket" (Rod Laver), "Newc" (John Newcombe), "Fiery " (Fred Stolle), and of course "Muscles" (Ken Rosewall). One of the best nicknames I thought was "Hanoi" (Terry Sanders)—he was bombed every night.

South Africa

So "Digger" and I headed for South Africa. First stop on the tour to nowhere. What a wonderful place to start the journey. Johannesburg was exciting, so foreign yet so British just like our Aussie cities. The only difference was that the black Africans outnumbered the Europeans five to one. That was weird, because I'd never seen too many Australian aboriginals let alone all these black Africans in one place.

The hospitality was amazing. Everyone was housed privately rather than in hotel accommodation. The whites seemed to have it made. They exuded wealth and confidence (arrogance?) and were waited on hand and foot by the natives. My digs were with the Roberts family. Doug Roberts was a very influential man and one of the richest men in South Africa (Roberts Construction constructed the Sydney underground railway project as well as other big developments in South Africa). He was also chairman of the iconic Wanderers Club in Johannesburg. The Roberts had a beautiful mansion, lawn tennis court, a Rolls Royce and a BMW, etc. plus a host of servants. My roommate was a Melbournian, John Brown, a seasoned pro. A bit older than me, JB was a good man to show a rookie the ropes. As it turned out our hosts were out of the country on a trip during the first week of the two-week tournament. The S.A. Open was the fifth major in the tennis world after the four slams, a fortnight event. We arrived very late the first night after possibly the longest trip in the flying world, Sydney to Perth, across the Indian Ocean (with a refuel in Mauritius) to Johannesburg. Absolutely dog tired and whacked out "Brownie" and I were escorted to our accommodation in fashionable Melrose. We were housed in a guest cottage away from the main living quarters. Because of the high break-ins and petty crime in Johannesburg everything was wired with alarms and patrolled by security guards. Not knowing of our exact arrival the Roberts had left the cottage wired up while they were out of the country. I was the first to enter the bungalow, the alarm was tripped and suddenly a huge Zulu man (I'm just saying Zulu, it sounds more warlike) appeared from out of the shadows. He was one second away from braining me. He held a massive donger over my head and was ready to beat my jet-lagged brain into pulp. Very luckily for me one of the house servants who was informed of our arrival that night yelled some order in Swahili or something and this giant black man lowered his weapon. Just imagine, I could have died on my first day out of the country, my tennis career over before it started. I visualised the headline in the Toowoomba Chronicle or the Courier Mail in Brisbane: "Young Australian Tennis Star killed in South Africa. He never hit a ball, poor guy".

The South African Open was a wonderful tournament. The promoter of the tournament, Owen Williams, did a great job. Owen was a former player and he knew how to woo the top players down to Johannesburg and he certainly produced a great show. He even looked like the consummate promoter/showman—tall and debonair, always immaculately dressed in his pinstriped suits, a big cigar constantly in place. Owen was very charming, as well. Many players wanted to play South Africa.

There were cocktail parties seemingly every day and night and private parties in peoples' mansions. Lots of beautiful people hung around the tennis. Owen had invited the world famous heart surgeon, Dr Christian Barnaard, to attend all the tennis functions. And his second successful transplant patient, Pieter Smith, came along and played in the tennis pro-am. I think Dr Barnaard was also breaking lots of women's hearts besides transplanting hearts.

The matches were played at the famous Ellis Park in Johannesburg. The thing that really hit me was the segregation of the fans in the stadium. This apartheid thing was weird. The stadium was divided into two sections, the non-white section (nie blanke) and the white section (blanke). The toilets or change rooms were divided into white and non-whites, just like the bus stops. I wonder where Arthur Ashe changed or went to the bathroom when he eventually visited South Africa to play tennis? It was hard to get your head around this apartheid thing.

Next year when I revisited Johannesburg, I played a doubles match with my tennis partner, Ross Case against a couple of legends, Laver and Gonzales. Rodney was the champion of everything in the world it seemed and he had won the Grand Slam the previous year. Even better he was a fellow Queenslander. Pancho was now the aging lion, the big cheese of the pro tour. At 41, he could still compete with the younger pros. We lost on that black and white stadium court but we took a set, which was a respectable result against the two legends.

In my debut singles match I was pretty sorrowful. The altitude of Johannesburg (5000+ feet) affected me. I felt like I had altitude sickness and my flat groundstrokes were knocking down the fences. I lost poorly to a regional South African player who was great on his home court. No excuses. It took me a week to become used to the altitude and I never did play in altitude again in other countries, like smoggy Mexico City or mile-high Denver, Colorado. Maybe I did play once in Teheran, which is also quite high. I even thought about asking Dr Barnaard for a new heart because mine did not seem to be working.

The second week of the tournament gave me some redemption because I reached the final of the 21 and under event and that had some good talent from Australia and South Africa in the field.

Another one of Owen Williams' coups during that first year was to invite the Wimbledon referee out to South Africa to run the tournament. Captain Mike Gibson was a big figure in the tennis world. He was ex Sandhurst, the famous military school for officer training in the army. Captain Gibson definitely looked the part, ramrod straight back, bristling moustaches and dressed like a General. You felt like you should salute first before addressing the Captain. He refereed many tournaments in England but mainly he was The Man at the All England Club. His word was gospel. Before the computer rankings were introduced after the Association of Tennis Professionals (A.T.P.) was formed the Captain literally decided who played at Wimbledon.

He was not the guy you pissed off if you were a fringe player. He would decide if you were in the tournament or relegated to the qualifying event.

The first time I addressed the Captain later on at a small English tournament, he glanced up from his desk to tell me when my match was scheduled: "Yes Gardiner, umm...two-ish, two-ish". Dismissed. I felt like saluting him. Yes, sah. His nickname became "Two-ish" amongst our circle of Aussies after that encounter.

One afternoon after tennis at Ellis Park I was heading back to my digs along with "Digger" Hammond. Captain Mike was also allocated to our chauffeur driven car although his housing was a bit farther out. He sat up front with the chauffeur, Timothy, a black African. He did not acknowledge the peasants in the back seat and just engaged himself in reading the Daily Telegraph. After a seemingly interminable time in the car it appeared Timothy was lost but he just kept driving on aimlessly. Finally the Captain turned to Timothy and said "Timothy, I say, where the devil are we?"

"Don't know, sah". We had quite a chuckle. The Captain may have ordered him to be flogged and definitely relegated to "Qualies".

Wow what a place to start my tennis journey. This was going to be fun if all the tournaments were like this. The players were treated like stars and every effort was made to make them comfortable. Owen Williams had really learned a lot from the Americans on how to put on a show.

In a couple of weeks reality would strike when we headed for England to play a series of tournaments leading up to Wimbledon in June. Soon, we would be in grey England at a small club in northern London. Waiting around for hours in the cold and wet to play a crappy match on a crappy all-weather court. Sitting in the miserable clubhouse, eating watercress or cucumber sandwiches and drinking endless cups of tea. Everything was grey, the sky, the buildings, even the spectators in their dark clothes, watching the matches braving the cold and inevitable drizzle, their brollies up. Matches continued in the drizzle otherwise the tournament would go on for a year, rather than for a week. Rarely were matches called off due to weather. There was very little prize money, no hospitality (except perhaps out of London in the county events). Rather frightful conditions actually.

This would be a far cry from that first tournament in South Africa.

Israel

But before England, the next stop was Israel.

We stopped off in the Promised Land for a couple of tournaments before the British season started. It was probably too cold and wet for the English tournaments so we were playing where there was a bit of sunshine.

My memories of Tel Aviv are the noise, the constant honking of car horns, uptight people and constant bedlam. I guess most

Middle Eastern cities are like that and the Arab cities like Cairo and Beirut are probably more chaotic. Other memories were of the whores plying their trade in the vacant lot by our hotel. We were there during Passover.

I was a bit hazy on the story of Passover, so I could not understand why breakfast always consisted of the unleavened matzah bread and boiled eggs?

Some years later I was in Israel again at Passover. We played at a small tournament down at Beersheba in the Negev desert. A few of the Aussies were housed at a Kibbutz in Beersheba and we were honoured to be invited to a seder, the ritual feast marking the beginning of Passover. To our delight, a special guest that night was the former Prime Minister of Israel, Golda Meir. Mrs Meir was such a big figure on the world stage, the first female leader of Israel and the heroine of the six-day Arab-Israeli war. Her daughter and son-in-law were residents of the Kibbutz. It was nice to chat to Mrs Meir and touching that we gentiles were part of their special night.

The tournament in Tel Aviv was quite small and played at a little club with dirt courts nestled amongst apartment buildings. A couple of years later the tournament relocated to a very nice new tennis centre at a place called Ramat Hasharon. Here I lost the singles final to a fellow Aussie and Queenslander, David "Space" Carter. David was a very quiet spoken guy, somewhat philosophical and pensive. Looked like he could have stepped out of biblical times. Later on he would adopt Israel as his home and join their Davis Cup squad. During that final of the Israel open, I won the match fair and square in three sets but the fans wanted to see some more tennis. The officials requested us to extend the match to the best of five sets. Bitterly, I recall, I had match points in the fourth set then lost the fifth. Oh well, there was not a great difference of prize money between winner and finalist but somehow I squandered a national title. King David had a better ring to it than King Alvin.

The following week we played down in Jerusalem. It seemed a little sacrilegious to be playing tennis in the Holy City. What an awe-inspiring old place. What history.

I was rooming with "Space" at the quite fashionable King David hotel in Jerusalem. One night we were asleep and a guy came into our room (for some reason our door was not locked, I blamed "Space" for that), walked around obviously a bit drunk and disorientated. Finally he climbed into bed with "Space" before realising this did not feel right. He found his way out mumbling in some foreign drunk tongue "A friend of yours?" I asked. "No. Actually, we're not that close. Goodnight Agg". Seemingly, nothing fazed the Spaceman.

Chapter 2
Off to Jolly England

I really did not understand why so many players descended on the Mother country during April and May each year. I guess the main reason was there were not too many places to play during that time of year. The big name players were probably on the US indoor circuit. The Europeans might be playing indoors still as well or playing a few outside tournaments in preparation for the French Open which was in May.

It appeared that the English circuit was made up of Aussies, Kiwis, South Africans and of course the local grown English guys and girls. A lot of the people just wanted to get some tournaments in before Wimbledon as they were on the fringe and to put in some good results to impress Captain Gibson and the Wimbledon committee.

Nobody wanted to be in the qualifying tournament before Wimbledon. That was for sub-humans. It was very nerve racking and very difficult to get through three matches under truly testing conditions. Yes, everything revolved around Wimbledon. It was the centre of the tennis world: the Tennis Mecca. Everybody played the big "W" or wanted to play the "Wimbie". However, the other big Grand Slam in Europe, the French Championships was also close to Wimbledon in time. Only about three weeks separated the two big ones. Just when you became accustomed to playing on clay, it was time to forget about slow clay courts and get accustomed to fast grass, a whole different game. Some of the players on the English tour would duck off to Paris for the French—not the best preparation though to go from the English shale courts to the much slower Continental clay. It was still dirt though, just different dirt.

I really enjoyed London. It was a fun city, easy to get around on the underground and things were fairly cheap. Also, so much better when everyone speaks English. I am sure London has changed in the present day, definitely not cheap and maybe not many people speaking the Queen's English.

In 1968 a few touring Aussie tennis players had discovered a nice Bed and Breakfast in Putney, London S.W. 15 and only two tube stops from Wimbledon down the road. This B&B was run by a Mrs Drake. She was English but had spent some of her younger days in India where her family were in the services. She definitely had a soft spot for the Colonials and welcomed all the Aussie tennis players at any time of year. It was no five star hotel by any means. But cheap, comfortable, and like a home away from home. She treated us like her boys. Mrs Drake never could pronounce my name throughout my five years staying there, off and on—it was always "Allwin" and I was still "Allwin" when I spent the good part of 1973 at the B&B recuperating from shoulder surgery.

It was quite amusing during the Wimbledon fortnight when the official courtesy cars from the All England Club would roll up to Mrs Drake's. In those early days the cars were grand old black Rolls Royces or Bentleys with the purple and green flag flying on the bonnet. Those who were competing in the tournament proper would be chauffeur driven to the "W". From our modest little B&B this seemed a tad incongruous.

We were also fortunate that there were a couple of inexpensive restaurants nearby and we were walking distance from Flannigan's Pub. That was a popular hangout for the Aussies in particular. Warm and weak beer but it went down well when the weather outside was cold and damp. We could stagger the short distance home and sometimes bring a couple of strays back to our digs.

One night "Digger" and I brought back two girls to Mrs Drake's B&B. Because we often shared two or three guys to a room, we wanted a little more privacy. As it turned out the number one room at the top of the stairs was vacant. It was most likely the best room in the place. A couple of the players, "JA" and "Philby" had checked out that morning for another tournament somewhere in Wales. So "Digger" and I and the girls sneaked into room number one, brought our portable music, a few drinks and were having a little party with lights out. Suddenly, there was a knock on the door. Apparently Mrs Drake had booked the room months before to an elderly couple, her friends from up country who would come once a year to spend time in London. This was their room all neat and prepared for them. We had been sprung. Sheepishly we sidled out of the room in a state of undress, girls in tow and mumbling our apologies to the new guests. It was a trifle embarrassing to say the least.

After some weeks of hacking around different parts of England the clay season would come to an end and the grass courts would open up. The early clay tournaments were fixtures at places like Cumberland and Paddington (in London), Sutton and Guildford (in Surrey), down to Bournemouth, Lee-on-Solent in the south, back to Norwich and other towns in the northern counties. These tournaments were quite strong with lots of foreign players around. The prize money was ludicrous, usually about $100 to win the whole thing. The weather was cold, invariably damp and drizzly. There were never many offers of hospitality especially in the tournaments in London but often in the smaller ones outside London. It was difficult to find practise courts and that seemed like lots of waiting around. Maybe you would get on court when the rains eased. Why did we play here? I'm not sure. Perhaps without the lure of Wimbledon around the corner, we would still be in Australia or finding tournaments that paid better in other parts of the globe.

But first it was time for Gay Paree...

Chapter 3

The French

I really thought that my four years of high school French would really help when I visited Paris. I was wrong. My concept of the language was quite OK on paper but conversationally it was a different story. The French seemed to speak so quickly and by the time I prepared my response they had moved on, way on. It seemed like they were speaking Swahili sometimes. I understood a lot and could manage the basics like ordering a meal or scoring a tennis match in French but forget the conversational French. We obviously did not practise enough French conversation in school classes. One needs total immersion I discovered.

This was my first time in a truly foreign country, a country where they speak a language other than English. I had now played in South Africa (bilingual of course) with English and Afrikaans, Israel (English and Hebrew) and the Motherland where they speak the Queen's English even though some dialects were difficult to understand.

The only problem with Paris was there were simply too many French people. They did not like other nationalities very much, just their own it seemed.

They did not like the Brits, or the Germans, which was understandable after the occupations. They disliked the Americans, too. I did not quite get that because the Americans and the Allies had come to their rescue in the war and the Americans liberated Paris. Australians? The French tolerated us because they did not know much about us. We were from somewhere on the other side of the world. However, there was a bit of tension between the governments of France and Australia sometime in the 1970s when Australia was upset, naturally enough, with the French atomic bomb tests in the south Pacific. I could not mail any letters to Australia from France for some time that summer.

My memories of Paris, The City of Light, are not of the famous attractions, the Louvre, Notre Dame, the Eiffel Tower, Les Champs Elysees, etc. but the simple things like the French breakfasts, the continental version of croissants and chocolat chaud (hot chocolate). It was all very quaint. The little sidewalk cafes serving espresso, the cobblestone streets, the juke boxes on the sidewalk—lots of Johnny Halliday, the French rock star in those times, and English singers as well. Everything seemed so expensive in Paris. You did not seem to get many francs for the US dollar or the English pound. However, I remember that first hotel in Paris where "Digger" and I stayed. It was cheap. A room at the Étoile (Star hotel) cost 25 francs, only about $US5. That was very cheap for the heart of Paris. Admittedly it was a shared room and came with a community bathroom but the price was right. Definitely a zero-star hotel was the hotel Étoile.

Everything else, besides our hotel in Paris, was expensive, especially the restaurants. We survived on much the same fare every night, usually steak avec pomme frites (chips) and petit pois (peas) and lots of baguette bread. I learned that the cheap steaks were probably steak au cheval, the horse kind. It was hardly exotic French cuisine but what could you do on a shoestring budget?

The iconic Stade Roland Garros was old and grey but nevertheless it seemed to ooze tennis history. I'm not sure why the stadium was named after the famous aviator, Roland Garros. Why not name it after a great tennis player from the past just like Australia did at the National tennis centre (Rod Laver Arena) or the US did at Flushing Meadows (Arthur Ashe stadium at the Billie Jean King tennis centre)? Maybe the French didn't have any great tennis heroes? How about calling it Stade René Lacoste after one of the four musketeers who were very famous and dominated the Davis Cup and the Major Championships for a time in the 1920s?

Roland Garros did seem old. Even the officials were old. The courts were the slow red clay, terre battue, set amongst the trees with some secluded courts here and there around the grounds like private enclosures. I have some nice memories of the little players' restaurant and eating those wonderful sandwiches de jambon and the musty old changing rooms with players chatting in various European languages. There were often sporadic cries to the Moroccan locker room guy: "Mabrouk, Mabrouk une serviette, s'il vous plait" (a towel, please).

The players all showed up for this tournament, Les Championats International de France or The French Championships, later to be simply called The French Open. The players just referred to it as the French.

The Iron Curtain had been parted for this major. Players came from all over Europe and the Eastern Bloc in particular. These players did not get to travel much but they certainly let them out for the French fortnight. There were Russians (Metreveli, Likhachev, Lamp, although Metreveli their star player was from Georgia in the USSR and he hated being called Russian); Hungarians (Taroczy, Baranyi, Szoke, Gulyas); Czechs (the big men Zednik, Holacek, and their great star Kodes); Poles (Gaziorek, Nowicki, Fibak); The Balkans (Pilic, Jovanovic, Spear); Romanians (the superstar Nastase, Tiriac) just to name some from behind the Curtain. Then, all the western Europeans were in attendance, the best players from West Germany (none from East Germany though), Sweden, Italy, Spain, Austria, Holland, etc. and the French players who were always going to be tough on their home courts. That was just the Europeans. There were always the contingent of Aussies, Brits and Americans who would try their hand on the slow stuff.

For me, this was my first time at a Grand Slam Tournament other than the Australian Championships. In those days, the Aussie Slam was comprised of probably 90% Australians and just a few overseas players from the USA or a few from Europe who would come down in the southern summer to play on the grass courts. It was a bit daunting in Paris because you knew that all these European players in particular were born and bred on the clay. The rallies could go on for days on the terre battue (literally, the beaten earth) or pulverised brick, which gave it the red texture. It was quite torturous especially when the weather was damp and the balls became very heavy. This was springtime in Paris but invariably the weather was cold and damp and the conditions were heavy.

I was looking forward to playing on this stuff having learned my tennis on the ant bed courts of Queensland. The ant bed courts were constructed from pulverised termite nests, rather than from smashed bricks, then rolled out for a compact surface. We played on those courts in most tournaments while the grass season was reserved for the big State and National titles during the summer. However, the European clay courts were much slower than our courts. Also the choice of balls was important. In earlier days the French Federation used Slazenger balls, which were pretty lively just like the balls they used on the grass at Wimbledon. When our great champion from Australia, Fred Stolle won the French in 1966 serving and volleying his way to the title the Frenchies became a little pissy then changed the balls to the Pirelli brand. This was like going from rockets to lead balloons and it gave the French guys a little better chance to win their National title.

At my first French I managed to qualify for the main draw, the tableau final which was a fairly pleasing effort without any lead up practice on the dirt. Qualifying in those days was three rounds, best of five sets in pre tie-breaker times. It seemed crazy to play three out of five sets in qualifying (same at Wimbledon) but it was in accordance with the main draw. The only good news was the optional ten-minute break after three sets. I was fit enough, but that's a long time hacking around in the red dirt getting covered with the gritty clay. In my second round qualifying match, against a "Froggie", I started to get leg cramps well into the third set. One of my Aussie buddies watching the match jumped out on the court and gave me a bit of a rubdown. That helped me to take out the third set, and then I jumped into a nice shower and a quick change of clothes during the obligatory ten-minute break. I came out cramp-free in the fourth set and finished off the match. In retrospect, I should have been disqualified for receiving on-court assistance. That should have been an automatic DQ (what was my friend thinking?). Surprisingly the French official and my French opponent did not protest. Nowadays it's common to have injury time outs and bathroom breaks.

My first match in the French was quite disappointing. I got hammered by an experienced European, the number three-ranked German. He was tough, but I was over-awed by the occasion and my opponent. "Digger" and I stayed in Paris for the whole two weeks of the championship. Usually players would skedaddle back to England as soon as they lost in Paris and get some invaluable grass court practice in the lead up tournaments to Wimbledon. However, we played in the doubles and I was invited to represent Australia in the junior singles (18 years and under). I did well but lost in the finals to one of the rising Spanish stars. Even then Spain had some great champions (namely the superstar Manolo Santana and the great Andres Gimeno) and Spain always produced champions at Roland Garros. They still do today of course with their superstar Rafa Nadal an extraordinary nine-time champion of Paris.

One of my early memories of the French Open was on finals day. "Digger" and I were practicing on the outer courts of Roland Garros when an older player came jogging down to our court with one racket in his hand politely asking if he could hit a few with us. Of course we recognised this smallish man with the perfectly combed Brylcream hair. It was Ken Rosewall a.k.a. "Muscles" or "God" to the other players. He was about to meet the great Rod Laver in the final in 30 minutes time. We were probably thinking this isn't much of a preparation for a Grand Slam final match. Perhaps it was just a little pre-match warm up before he went out on the stadium court.

We had heard about Laver's legendary practice sessions of two to four hours before a match. That seemed a ridiculous amount of preparation prior to a best of five set match but the "Rocket" was a notoriously slow starter in some of his matches and he felt that he needed this prep.

Anyway I hope our hit with Kenny hadn't caused him to lose the final to Laver. Laver was destined to win that 1969 final and the other three Grand Slam finals to complete his second career Grand Slam. These two guys had met in the previous year in the final, the first Open in 1968. Rosewall had won that one, his second French title after a 14-year break. He had won there as a youngster in the 1950s, turned pro with Jack Kramer, then came back to win it again when tennis was opened up to everyone. What an achievement, winning a major then repeating it 14 years later.

One little highlight of my first French open tournament was visiting the House of Lacoste. Lacoste tennis clothing was the coolest gear you could wear in those days. The crocodile logo was the epitome of fashion in the world of tennis and the French, of course, made clothing with style. Players in the main draw of Paris were entitled to an issue of clothing—shorts, shirts, vests and sweaters. The House of Lacoste was situated in the fashionable Rue de Castiglione close to the Place de la Concorde. It was started by René Lacoste back in the heyday of the Musketeers and was still run by another Musketeer, "Toto" Brugnon who would greet each player as they came into the store. And the other Musketeer,

Monsieur Borotra, the "Bouncing Basque" was still an avid tennis fan and one of the personalities around Roland Garros.

There sure wasn't much prize money to be won in 1969 so getting our Lacoste issue was exciting. Just imagine the champions in the pre 1968 open era receiving a trophy, some tennis gear and a pat on the back. Knock yourself out. Nowadays, the men's and women's champion collect about $US2 million to win the singles in each Slam plus a gazillion dollars in endorsements. Open tennis has come a long way but I was really happy to get some cool gear for free.

That was my first French. I went back to Paris quite a lot of times but never did much damage on the dust. You tend to recall some of your wins and (conveniently) forget a lot of your losses.

One of my matches in Paris brings back vivid memories of a loss that hurt me a bit. It was 1977 and my A.T.P. ranking was quite healthy at the time, good enough to be accepted in the main draw without going through that abominable qualifying. By this time the qualifying matches were reduced to two out of three sets rather than the old best of five sets. But no one wanted to go through that nerve racking "Qualies" where to lose in any of the rounds meant bye, bye, au revoir and zero prize money. It was all or nothing, glory or goner.

My opponent who I was drawn to play that year turned out to be one of the 16 qualifiers. That's a good draw usually and always better than playing B. Borg the number one seed who was virtually invincible on clay. He was the Rafa Nadal of the 1970s. My qualifying opponent turned out to be a young kid, just turned 18 and fresh out of high school: John McEnroe. That name did not conjure any fear then like the thought of playing Borg on clay. We had heard of this young guy who was to win the National Collegiate Athletic Association (NCAA) Championships as a freshmen at Stanford College. That's pretty heady stuff to be that good in your first year of college. Only Jimmy Connors had also achieved that feat, to win the National title in the first year competing in the college championships.

Still that was a good draw, I thought. To play an American on clay was usually an encouraging draw because the Americans generally play all their tennis on fast hard courts in the USA. Some could not break an egg on clay. Little did I know that "Mac" had played a lot of tennis on the clay courts (the faster "har tru" surface) during his formative years at the Port Washington Tennis Academy in New York City, his hometown. He had come over that spring to play some tournaments still playing as an amateur while having a crack at the French and Wimbledon tournaments.

His final round opponent in the qualifying was a buddy of mine, Bob Rheinberger from country New South Wales. "Rhino" was a bit of a self-made player with a workman-like game but quite useful on clay. He was pretty much tooled by this kid in the final qualifying round: the score was fairly easy. I had a chat to "Rhino" after his match and he reassured me that I would be OK, he was not that impressed with the kid and mentioned his forehand was a bit dodgy, as well. You'll be right, he said. Thanks for the vote of confidence mate.

We played our match on one of the more obscure courts at Roland Garros. No linesmen in those days, well not for our match anyway. The central umpire, our only umpire, was a Frenchman of course. Only a few spectators, a few of my friends watched the match and maybe one dog, as well. I don't think Mac had any friends there. He didn't make many friends on court that day, either. I remember leading 4-1 in the opening set. Mac became irritated about something—maybe a dicey line call or a dog was moving in the crowd—and stopped play for a while. He seemed to play much better after a break and letting off some steam: first set 6-4 McEnroe.

Second set, same scenario. I led 4-1 again, two service breaks this time, feeling confident now and assured of this set. Once again,

Mac stopped play for quite a long period, bitching and ranting some more. The umpire (no English in him) stepped down from his chair to settle things with this young American and to validate his line calls. Often in the French Championships umpires would jump down and point to a mark on the clay, usually to much whistling and jeering from the crowd. I moved towards the umpire's chair to see what was going on and suggested to Junior that it was best to keep playing because the umpire did not understand New York speak or any of his expletives for that matter. Mac's reply to me: "You shut the fuck up!" After a few minutes of this pointless arguing, he came roaring back playing like a man possessed. Score: second set 6-4 McEnroe.

I was deflated. There I was down two sets to one to this little jerk with big hair and a red headband. But I am thinking, hey, I should be leading 2-0 not trailing 2-0. Unfortunately in my early days out there on the tour I was a bit of a mental midget. I could guts it out physically and play for a week but mentally I was not so strong.

The third set against McEnroe was a tank job, 6-0 to McEnroe. Final score: 6-4, 6-4, 6-0. It was a pretty poor effort for the final set, my six-year old boy could have definitely done better. That was very un-Australian of me not to go to war with the kid and to stay out and win at all costs even if things became ugly, which they did. Fight in the trenches mate. Never give up.

McEnroe's next opponent in the French draw was Phil Dent, one of our leading Aussies on any surface and a Davis Cup star. "Philby" was in great form reaching the semi-finals of the Italian Open in Rome the previous week beating Nastase (probably the best clay court player on the planet until B. Borg arrived) along the way. The match was a centre court duel. Phil squeaked it out in five sets and the kid pushed him to the limit. Out of character, McEnroe gave a point to Phil at a critical stage of the final set, actually reversing one of the umpire's calls. That was probably a first and last time for Mac.

But Junior had arrived. Two weeks later he qualified again at Wimbledon winning three matches in "Qualies" and then went all the way to the semi-finals beating Sandy Mayer (one of the top Americans) and then "Philby" in the quarters. Phil said to me later "I had a tough time on the clay with him but I was very confident to take him on my surface, grass". That did not happen. He then gave Jimmy Connors a great four set battle in the semi- final. What a debut. He won eight matches on the grass and I'm not sure if he had seen grass before that tournament. McEnroe was good on any surface, even on chewing gum, I reckon.

So as it evolved, I was McEnroe's first victim in a Grand Slam event. This was his first singles match in a Slam. He was still an amateur. In his book *You Cannot Be Serious* (with James Kaplan, published 2002), Mac recalled his first Slam match opponent, Alvin Gardiner, an Aussie Journeyman who gave him few problems in his first round match. However, his on court attitude gave me some problems.

Yeah, I think that he was right, only a journeyman would have given it a tank when things went bad. I was utterly disappointed losing to an inexperienced young American on clay. I had blown what seemed like a great opportunity to advance in the French Championships.

To add insult to injury McEnroe did not look like a great athlete or player. His technique was a bit quirky. This kid must have been great at geometry and chess at school because he appeared to know every angle, every dimension of the court, and to think a couple of shots ahead of his opponent. What a strange serving style. Plus he did not look like he could run fast. Not even a suntan. And who wears a red headband anymore? But we were soon to learn, and quite soon, what a genius he was with a racquet. He moved extremely well, his lefty serve was a lethal weapon and he had an uncanny knowledge of the court. He knew what shots to play and had an array of power shots and deft volleys. And the more pissed off he became his level of play was raised (shades of the great Gonzales who had that same rage and ability to harness the rage).

McEnroe won all the Slams but was denied the French Open. He definitely could play on dirt and "should have, could have" won the 1984 final losing to Ivan Lendl. He was giving Lendl a drubbing, up two sets to love, easily, plus a break in the third when the points became a little more difficult and he went ape over some line calls. Lendl finally prevailed in five sets for his first Grand Slam singles title. McEnroe never did win the French. That must still hurt him today. I don't think he had any respect for Lendl even on clay where Lendl was to be the King for a long time.

Maybe he thought Lendl was a journeyman too.

After Paris it was time to get back across the channel to sunny England and prepare for the big "W"- Wimbledon.

Chapter 4

Wimbledon

The whole tennis world revolved around Wimbledon: the Holy Grail. It was the high point of the tennis year and definitely The Tournament. The All England Club in Church Road, Wimbledon, is a very private London club where they play croquet and tennis. In the understated British way, they call the tournament The Championships. In a similar fashion, the British Open golf championships, the oldest of golf's majors, is simply known as The Open. Wimbledon has been around forever, I think about 135 years. That's a lot of tradition. I was fortunate enough to play the singles in the centenary Wimbledon of 1977. Each competitor received a beautiful engraved pen set from the All England Club (so I do have a Wimbledon trophy of sorts). This was the tennis Mecca. Everyone wanted to make the pilgrimage to Wimbledon: the big "W" or " Wimbie".

A few lead up tournaments existed between and during the French Open and Wimbledon. There were only a few weeks to get used to grass after the slow clay of the Continent. It seemed like a different game: the grass surface was so fast and treacherous, often with irregular bounces, very slippery when wet which was often the case in England. The serve was king. With a good serve and volley you would be hard to beat on this stuff. Just like in Paris, the weather conditions could play a big factor. During the first week of the Championships, the courts were still lush and soft. No one had played on these courts all year until now. If the sun did come out (occasionally), the courts would play differently in the second week. The grass would get a little dried out with some bare patches and the ball bounce would be higher. The trick was to last till the second week. The great Borg did not enjoy the low bounce of the first week but being a champion he survived somehow and then the higher bounce later on really suited his game. He won the thing five straight times and grass was not his bag.

Prior to Wimbledon the regular grass events were in places like Surbiton (Surrey) and Beckenham (Kent) during the French fortnight. Then there was Nottingham and Manchester up north and Eastbourne down on the south coast for the girls. The final warm-up tournament was at the Queens Club in West London. Just called Queens it was for the elite men those who had direct acceptances into the Wimbledon draw.

The other poor buggers, the sub-humans, had to go through the ordeal of qualifying. It was a weeklong tournament held the same time as Queens. The venue was the Bank of England Club in Roehampton only four miles from Wimbledon in the south west part of London. Conveniently it was only a five minute ride from our base, Mrs Drake's B&B in Putney.

The Wimbledon draw is 128 men. However only 104 receive direct acceptance, 16 come from the qualifying tournament and eight are wildcards awarded by the All England committee to total 128 main draw players.

The Bank of England club was quite an exclusive club. Its a beautiful facility with indoor heated swimming pools, soccer fields, etc. and wonderful changing rooms. But no tennis courts Amazingly the tennis courts were marked out on the soccer pitch sometime in May or June. They simply ran some chalk lines on the grass, put up nets and some teeny enclosures and suddenly you had about a dozen courts all in a line down the pitches. A bit rinky-dink for Wimbledon, I would have thought, but this was not Wimbledon, yet. The so-called sub-humans had to go through the rigours of Roehampton. It was all or nothing. If you fell at one of the three stages of qualifying, it was over. If you survived the Q school you achieved the glory of playing at the All England Club. You were upgraded to human status. Welcome to Mecca.

Everyone was tough at Roehampton. You had to have a pretty good standing just to get into "Qualies". In the early days, pre A.T.P. and the computerised world rankings, acceptance was done on National rankings and how Captain Gibson, the Wimbledon referee and the Wimbledon Committee judged your standing. Pretty much Captain Gibson was the man: a good guy to have on your side. A favourable draw at qualifying was more likely a European or a South American opponent, the clay courters. They had not seen too much grass in their day. The Australians and Brits had much more experience on grass and the Americans and South Africans were very capable on fast surfaces, mainly hard courts, and they adapted quickly to grass. But on the courts of Roehampton, where the bounces could be very bad, the weather horrible, cold and often wet, anybody was tough on a slippery grass court/soccer field. To beat your grandmother in her walker was a good win at "Qualies". So here it was, Sydney or the bush.

In 1969, my first time at the dreaded Roehampton, I had a good win over a top Englishmen in the first round. That was a pretty good win, a bit of an upset, because this guy was very "useful" as the Brits love to say. Second round, not so useful on my part because I lost to a clay courter, a German player. Who said the Europeans were no good on grass? The Germans were not known for their grass court powers but that all went out the window when wunderkind Boris Becker appeared on the scene in 1985 and won the whole damn thing as a teenager. Boris's game was made for grass.

So that was it, was my first attempt at the big "W". "Digger" and I did not qualify in the men's doubles. I can't even remember the match (but that was the golden rule, forget your losses and just move on. Only remember your wins).

In those early days we would enter the mixed doubles as well. If you nabbed a half decent partner, you could almost sneak a direct acceptance. And getting into the mixed draw meant all the perks of Wimbledon. That earned you the all important competitors badge, which entitled you to free meals in the players' tearoom and strawberries and cream till you burst. The only down side to the mixed competition was you did not receive tickets to centre court and court number one. Those tickets were invaluable in getting friends into Wimbledon, especially into the show courts. Another down side to the mixed was it did not start until the second week and invariably the matches could get backlogged due to weather. A lot of players gave it the nice, friendly tank so they could get out of town. The girl partner hopefully understood the situation or you discreetly mentioned you had a plane reservation. There was very little prize money involved so that influenced the decision to lose gracefully and get out of town.

It would be disappointing to miss out on playing singles but we still had a chance to see the whole spectacle of Wimbledon, hang out in the players' tearoom and see some wonderful matches. One of the most enthralling matches I have ever seen anywhere was that year on centre court. The centre court was such an intimate setting and charged with atmosphere. Not a huge stadium but you felt really close to the battle.

The first round saw the ageing Pancho Gonzales (then 40 years old) playing Charlie Pasarell (a US Davis Cup star and former number one in USA). Charlie was involved in three consecutive epic matches in a row at Wimbledon. Firstly, he knocked off the defending champion Manolo Santana of Spain in the 1967 opener and then played a classic losing match to Ken Rosewall in that first Open Wimbledon the following year. Now in 1969 he had yet another first round battle royal with arguably the best player ever before the open era, Gonzales.

Pancho ranted and raged (à la McEnroe) through the opening day. They were sent on court in the twilight hours of the first day, a bit late to start a best of five-match even though there was daylight until 9:30 or later at night in June. Pasarell won the first two sets 24-22, 6-1. This was before the tie-breaker was introduced. Even then the Brits played the breaker at eight games all rather than six games all. The Wimbledon referee, Captain Gibson, had been summoned to the centre court midway through the second set when the light was fading. Gonzales' eyes were older than Pasarell's eyes, so he wanted to call it for the day. What was the point of continuing, they could not possibly complete the match that day even if it only went three sets. "Play on, gentlemen" said the Captain. Gonzales was pissed off, as he often was on court.

He virtually tanked the last couple of games and the second set. Along with a bit of racquet throwing and cursing, he stormed off the court.

At the end of day one the usually reserved British crowd booed Pancho off the centre court. That was unheard of on centre.

The next afternoon they resumed the match with lots of daylight available. Gonzales prevailed in five memorable sets winning the last three sets 16-14, 6-3, 11-9. What a marathon. 112 games of tennis, the longest in games ever played ever at Wimbledon (until the record was shattered in 2010) these men were like gladiators in the colosseum. Twice the old man was down 0-40 in the fifth set, facing seven match points in all, and each time he saved the "matchies" with a delicate drop volley or some other deft shot. Pancho won on sheer guts and determination. These guys were like heavy weight boxers plugging away in the 15th round.

The centre court crowd gave a standing ovation, which seemed to go on for minutes. They had forgiven Gonzales his misdemeanours of the previous evening. It wasn't the highest quality tennis match I have witnessed but it was definitely one of the most drama filled, emotional tennis battles ever seen anywhere, and especially on that hallowed turf.

One would have thought their record 112 games in a match would last eternally, especially with the advent of the tie-breaker not long afterwards. But in 2010, John Isner, the giant American, beat Frenchmen Nicholas Mahut in a titanic battle, the final set taking eight hours to play! That set in itself was three hours longer than the entire Gonzales v Pasarell match. The fifth set was 70-68. That is just ridiculous. I had never heard of a set over 30-28. Ever. Anywhere. (The final set was played until a two game advantage at W—no tie-breaker). Surely those guys staged this set to get into the record books. It does not seem possible otherwise.

1970 saw me at dreaded Roehampton once more, this time I'd battled through to the final round, the qualifying round. This is to make it into the men's singles main draw. My opponent in the last match was the British prodigy, Steven Warboys. Warboys was a snotty kid from an aristocratic family, an only child who was being groomed as the next great champion of Britain. The Brits had not had a Wimbledon singles champion in the men's division since the great Fred Perry who won it three in a row in the late 1930s. Stephen was OK off the court but he had such a cocky swagger on the court, you just felt like kicking him in the butt. The English press loved him. One of his comments, I read once, was that his goals were to win Wimbledon (admittedly a fair enough dream), to win the British Open, (the Wimbledon of Golf) and to be an international playboy à la James Bond. Stephen Warboys. Wow.

I wanted to smack him and tell him to get real.

In our encounter, Warboys won the first set 18-16, again before the tie-breaker was introduced a couple of years later. That set took about two hours. It was an unusually warm summer day in London. I lost the second easily 6-1. It was a bit of an emotional letdown after the long first set. But this was best of five sets and

I bounced back well, took the next two sets, and then levelled at 5-5 in the final set. See, this felt like Gonzales v Pasarell except we were on court number nine at Roehampton soccer field, not centre court at the All England Club.

We were the only match remaining on court for the final qualifier slot. During most of the match for 4½ hours we were alone except for one umpire (no linesmen), one ball boy, one spectator and Jack Warboys (Stephen's dad). Now there was quite a crowd of spectators to see this battle end.

At 5-5, 30-40 Warboys held a break point. This was like a virtual match point because, if he broke, I was not likely to break him on that fast, irregular bouncing court. We had not being doing much damage against each other's serves all day.

At break point I hit a good first volley right near the baseline for a winner. The baseline was a little smeared by this stage, chalk dust everywhere, but the volley was a few inches inside and too good for Warboys. The central umpire, Laurie McCallum, had done a good job all this time but, inconceivably, now he froze on this one. He did not call deuce but was undecided what to do, in or out? Both players knew the ball was in. At this time, Jack Warboys jumped out of his chair and yelled: "The ball was out". Mr McCallum decided to go with Stephens's Dad and called the shot out. Rather than replaying the point as he was undecided, he suddenly called "Game Warboys. Warboys leads six games to five final set". I was in deep shock. How could the umpire make this huge decision based on someone's call from the crowd, especially from my opponent's dad? I went a little ape and called for the referee, Fred Hoyles, the assistant Wimbledon referee to Captain Gibson. In the meantime, until he was summoned, the umpire is telling me to play on, Mr Gardiner, or you will be disqualified. Without the luxury of Hawkeye in the 1970s, all Mr Hoyles could do was go with the umpire's call. I was devastated as I went around to the other side and tried in vain to break Warboy's serve for the match, but the match was over, 18-16, 6-1, 4-6,4-6,7-5.

I needed McEnroe with me. You cannot be serious!! I had just been totally screwed. Later, I found out Laurie and Jack were buddies, the leading officials from their County tennis association. Laurie was peeing in Jack's pocket, so to speak.

I was utterly shattered, my arse was gutted. Wimbledon singles was over for me. The most devastating loss of my career I am sure. How could I go so close and be cheated at the finish line? Mr Hoyles was quite nice. He had been told what had actually happened by the players who were watching our match but he was powerless to change the umpire's decision. He consoled me in the dressing room (in case I slashed my wrists) and I could tell he genuinely felt for me. A few years later somewhere else in the tennis world, Mr Hoyles apologised for how I had been taken out so blatantly.

An hour later I was back on court with partner, Ross Case, for our second round qualifying doubles. We won in four sets. Then back on court for mixed doubles, the insurance event for that priceless competitors badge if everything else failed. I cannot remember who my poor partner was, but we lost in three sets. So on that very warm summer day in London, I had played 12 sets of tennis. Admittedly, the points are fairly quick on grass, but that was a lot of tennis. I think the nervous tension also was very draining and of course so was the physical effort. That was the most beaten up I had ever been after a day of tennis anywhere. It ranks with my maiden marathon years later—I was so knackered then I could not even get my shoes off without help and tears were rolling down my face from the exhaustion.

Ross and I did get through in doubles quite comfortably. Our first match at Wimbledon we lost to the top Russians, Metreveli and Likhachev on court number five but it was a thrill to be there, nevertheless. First match at Wimbledon for me, singles or doubles.

Ross and I did not play Wimbledon again together. No, he did not ditch me because of that match. A year or so later he was selected in the Australian Davis Cup team on his impressive singles results. I did not make the Davis Cup squad, so captain Neale Fraser decided to pair Ross with fellow Queenslander, Geoff Masters, also on the Davis Cup team. (All three of us had come up together in the junior ranks). Case-Masters became a great doubles team and they reached the Wimbledon final in 1976, then went all the way the next year, the centenary Wimbledon, beating Alexander-Dent in an all Aussie grand final. They became one of the great doubles teams in the tennis world. When I finally qualified in singles after the Warboys debacle my first round opponent was a gentleman and very nice guy from Rhodesia (now Zimbabwe), Hank Irvine. I didn't care if our match was on the last Court, number 16, or I was consigned to the dressing room B with the lesser minions, I was happy to get the Roehampton monkey off my back.

We played a pretty tight match. Both of us were as nervous as kittens.

Deep in the fifth set on a very crucial point I chose to hit a top-spin backhand passing shot. I had never hit one before in my life. I don't know what came over me. I always sliced my backhand like my hero, Ken Rosewall. Ken had arguably the best backhand known to mankind and he always sliced it, but that was Rosewall. I must have lost my mind because that was not the norm to come over my backhand à la Rod Laver. I think my passing shot hit the back canvas adjacent to a lineman's head !Then I proceeded to lose 9-7 in the fifth set. A fairly good singles debut but still a first round loss. After Wimbledon was over I learned the major sponsor of the Men's Grand Prix Tour that year, Commercial Union Insurance, had given a £1,000 prize to the best contested singles match of Wimbledon. Apparently the vote came down to two matches, Rosewall v Orantes or Gardiner v Irvine. Rosewall had beaten Orantes in a classic duel between two extraordinary shot makers, two great champions. Sadly for us the nod went to their match. We were not names but our match was surely a close contest. I could have definitely used £500. A first round loser received only £50 at that time. Currently it's a tidy £29,000. Ironically Rosewall and Orantes were both richer than I could imagine. Anyway we did well to make the final. The money in Wimbledon or any Slam back in those days was quite paltry but it would grow. Why wasn't I born in the 1970s rather than the 1950s?

In the Wimbledon qualifying competition there was no prize money. Nothing. It was three rounds of zero, zilch. Sydney or the bush—that was Q school. Thanks for coming. First round money in those days was not great but it would grow as Open tennis grew.

Prize Money 1970:
Qualies: all three rounds: £0
First round loser: Main Draw: £50
Tournament Winner: £2,000

Current Day Prize Money:
Qualies: 1st round loser: £3,375
3rd round loser: £13,500
Maindraw: 1st round loser: £29,000
Men's and Women's Tournament Winners : £2,000,000.
(Equal prize money).

I visited Wimbledon a few more times in the ensuing years as a singles player and as a doubles player. Sometimes, I was a direct acceptance in singles, sometimes a qualifier and once amazingly a wildcard. Traditionally the All England Lawn Tennis committee has allocated their eight wildcard spots to their local British hope-fuls (understandably so) and occasionally to a great player who had been out due to injury and whose ranking had suffered. In 1975 the Committee decided to give the wildcards to the singles winners in the small tournaments (on hard courts) leading up to the grass court season before Wimbledon. As it eventuated that year there were eight individual tournament winners. I was one of the fortunate bastards (winner at Lee-on-Solent) along with another Aussie, Peter McNamara (who went on to become a dual Wimbledon doubles champion). There were not two more surprised guys than Peter Mac and myself when we received out official letters from Wimbledon that year. No "Qualies" for us thankyou very much. It didn't do much good because I was hammered by one of the top ranked Americans in the first round. Perhaps the All England Club should give some sort of medal for the most first round losses there. I might be a contender.

All the same I was honoured to receive the wildcard and to avoid the horrors of Roehampton. That was the first and last time to date the club went with that system for wildcard allocation.

So that was "Wimbie". I loved the place. Everything was so British, so understated. They knew how to put on a show, the Brits, and they have been doing it for over 130 years. So much tradition, you could almost smell the history here.

I only regret I did not do better in the tournament. Perhaps I put too much pressure on myself and consequently did not perform to my potential.

I did see some historic matches. Normally, I can't sit through an entire tennis match—I'll watch a set at most and then move on—but I did see a few great men's singles finals in their entirety. It was sort of fun to sit in the players box, quite close to the royal box, and see those memorable matches. I was there for Rod Laver's win over John Newcombe in 1969 in his second career Grand Slam, Newcombe beating Rosewall in 1970, and Stan Smith in 1971, and also Stan's epic win over Ille Nastase in 1972—a five set battle. I saw the seemingly invincible Jimmy Connors crushing Ken Rosewall (then 40 years old) in the 1974 final, then losing the next year against Arthur Ashe. Arthur upsetting Jimmy against all odds it seemed.

I remember watching Bjorn Borg in those early 1970s struggling on the grass. He had conquered the French Open, losing there only twice in eight appearances. But his topspin game and vulnerability at the net made him look awkward on the grass. All the players agreed he was the king of the clay no question, but everyone figured he would never do well on the green stuff. Well he proved everyone wrong, winning Wimbledon five consecutive times from 1976 to 1980 and then barely losing the final to John Mac in 1981. Amazingly he could adapt to this alien surface and win against the traditional big serving grass courters. One year, when he was 16, I played Borg in the warm up grass court tournament at Beckenham down the road in Kent. It was the semi-finals of the secondary singles event, the 21 & under championships. I had heard of this kid who had debuted in Davis Cup for Sweden at age 15 and was beating everybody on dirt. But surely not on grass? I was quite confident to take him with my experience on grass courts against his perfect clay court game. He beat me 6-4, 6-4, and then won the final. I was sort of shocked at how nonchalant he seemed on court and how nerveless he appeared. When it was a break point, for example, he would invariably come up with an ace, sometimes a second serve ace (his serve was very good, no one talked that much about his great serve) and often he hit the line as well. He was really annoying. He looked so casual. What an athlete. Probably the best athlete to play the game, the quickest guy on two legs, (with some competition from Vitas Gerulaitis, Michael Chang and Johann Kriek in that era)

The best year of opportunity at Wimbledon was 1973. This was the boycott year, when about 70 guys, members of a newly formed Association of Tennis Pros (A.T.P.) walked out on the eve of Wimbledon.

It was all over the Nikki Pilic affair. Pilic had fallen out with the International Lawn Tennis Federation (I.L.T.F.) because he had refused to play Davis Cup for his country, Yugoslavia. It was probably over money (as it usually is) and he sustained a suspension from the I.L.T.F., which sanctioned the Grand Slam tournaments.

He was being prevented from playing Wimbledon and henceforth pursuing his livelihood. The union of the A.T.P. stood behind their member Nikki and threatened to strike at Wimbledon if he was not reinstated in the tournament. It came to any impasse on the eve of "Wimbie" after the draw had been done. Suddenly 70 or so were missing from the 104 direct acceptances. I think only two members reneged on the boycott and decided to play and not support the A.T.P. Two of the big stars of the game, Nastase and Connors were not members and consequently they played. The final was a pretty tame anticlimactic match between Jan Kodes from Czechoslovakia and Alex Metreveli from Georgia (USSR). None of the communist bloc players were A.T.P. members, either.

So to complete the draw of 128 men after the mass withdrawal, a lot of guys were pulled out of the Roehampton "Qualies" and upgraded to human status. What a present for them. Sadly I was sitting in Mrs Drake's B&B brooding because I was out of action with an injury. I had a bone graft operation on my clavicle that February (in Wimbledon Hospital of all places) and was still recuperating, very, very slowly. It was not a good year to miss Wimbledon. Very frustrating but stuff happens. There would always be another year to have a crack at the big "W".

Chapter 5

Bush Beginning

I was born in the bush. My birthplace was Tara, a nondescript little town in South East Queensland, probably two or three thousand inhabitants. Not sure what Tara is noted for, not much I guess, it just served farming and grazing communities in the area and further west. If the State of Queensland was shaped like a bull you would find Tara just under the bull's tail. Luckily though for me Tara did have a hospital. Not so lucky for my older brother Phil, though. Four years earlier, allegedly, he was born in the back of an old sulky (a cart drawn by a horse) near the town of Goondiwindi, which is further south than Tara. He did not have the luxury of a hospital. Apparently my Dad and Mum spent some time near "Gundy" where my Dad worked on a property. Later they bought some land, about 5000 acres, roughly 25 miles west of Tara.

Our home was Hannaford, just a little village with a post office, general store and a railway stop. Down the road a bit was a one-roomed school and adjacent to the school was the community centre. The centre had a big dance hall, a cricket ground and four ant bed tennis courts where I was to first see the wonderful game of tennis played.

I recall Hannaford was named after Samuel Hannaford in his vanity. He was one of those intrepid pioneers who passed through on his endless exploring journey to nowhere. He must have thought how average this country looked (although he did lend his name to it), just miles of bush country with lots of scrubby brigalow, a tree native to this area. Monster tractors pulling huge chains between them were used to clear the brigalow making the land perfect for raising sheep.

My Dad and his brother, my uncle Ken, shared this spread of 5000 acres. They had the arduous job of clearing the brigalow bush (with the tractors help of course), had some water dams dug, making the land suitable for growing grass and raising sheep. It was semi-arid land. Unfortunately the land was shared with lots of native animals: wild pigs, kangaroos, wallabies, goats and foxes. Too many kangaroos and the grass would be devoured in no time. It is quite interesting Australia has a 90 million population of kangaroos, roughly four times the human population.

I'm not exactly sure when tennis appeared in my life. I do know sport (along with drinking beer) was a big part of community life. Tennis and cricket were the sports of choice.

I would like to say I dreamed about Wimbledon and the Davis cup but that's not true. I don't think I had heard about this mysterious Wimbledon place until years later. We did not have electricity and, hence, no television growing up in Hannaford in the 1950s. However I do remember vividly listening to the big cricket matches, the Tests, on our little radio. Wimbledon did not exist for me yet. Later on in my teens I heard the radio reports coming from London by Alf Chave, a nice man who reported tennis on radio and for the Brisbane Courier Mail. He was the main man for snippets from Wimbledon each day of the fortnight.

More than likely my dream then was to be a great cricket player, to play test cricket for Australia. Now that is a dream. The best cricketer in the history of the game, Don Bradman, was a country boy like me. Why couldn't I be like the Don? I knew of Bradman, I had not heard of Sedgman, Rosewall and Laver yet. Apparently my Dad was a very good fast bowler growing up in the Sydney area. However the Second World War came around and that was the end of his career in cricket. He was also injured during the War years. He had enlisted for the Light Horse, an elite cavalry-like band of men famous in both World Wars. These were extraordinary men who fought the Turks and the Germans in the deserts of North Africa and Arabia during both World Wars. The ultimate battle was the taking of Beersheba (I played a tennis tournament once in Beersheba during a visit to Israel—a casualty in the quarter finals) charging in on horseback facing thousands of Turks who were entrenched and armed with machine guns: a bit like Gallipoli but with a better outcome. They were brave men. Unfortunately (or fortunately, maybe) my Dad did not make it to North Africa or the Middle East. He was breaking in horses for the Light Horse brigade before they headed overseas when he had both his knees crushed in an accident. That ended his chances of opening the fast bowling for Australia. He must have had some nerve though going into the ring to break a wild horse.

I enjoyed watching the big boys, the local men who played cricket at Hannaford oval. My uncle Ken was a good cricket player as were my other two uncles (dad's in-laws) from northern New South Wales. But the young kids in Hannaford did not have much chance to actually play a game of cricket. Well, not at school. Sometimes we had an opportunity to get out on the field and fill in a game with the men. Apart from that it was only a little backyard cricket. My older brother Phil had gone away to school so that left my younger sisters, Jan and Susan. I would coerce them into bowling to me (I loved to bat all the time) for hours on end. When they started crying I knew they were pissed off and had had enough of cricket and of me. After all it wasn't really a game girls played back in those days.

Tennis I could pretty much play anytime. Well, at least when we were down at the community centre which was about seven miles away from my house. And the little school was a lob from those four ant bed courts. In those days all the tennis courts around the country were generally ant bed and then grass in the southern States. Ant bed? Who would have thought ants had beds. No, the court was just a levelled area, covered in the granite from crushed termite nests. Those little hillocks of granite could be seen dotted around the countryside. When crushed then rolled with a heavy roller it made a perfect tennis surface. Throw in some chalk lines and you had a beautiful court. A little like the terre battue (literally the beaten earth) of Roland Garros in Paris and the courts all over continental Europe. The basic difference was the red courts of Europe were made from crushed bricks, not from annihilated ant nests.

I can still remember watching the adults play in the tournaments at Hannaford as well as in social games. Seemed like everyone played tennis in their spare time. My Dad played some but those old knees were buggered. I can't remember my Mum playing. She was not the sporty type but had immense talents with artist brushes and with the sewing machine.

I was in awe of how the good the bush players were. They all looked like stars, like pros dressed in their all white gear and canvas tennis shoes called sandshoes, swinging wooden rackets strung with catgut. I wanted to be one of them except I did not own any sandshoes. Barefoot all those years, I would go off to school without any kind of shoes. You tend to get some tough assed soles on your feet, sliding around on gravelly ant bed courts. I do admit to having a pair of old dusty sandshoes. These were reserved for going up the bush when my Dad would muster sheep or when we would go out to shoot wild boar. It was pretty much impossible to wander barefoot in the paddocks because the prickles (burrs) would kill you. Those burrs were so nasty even the sheep dogs would be yelping in pain from them.

Yes, there was lots of tennis at Hannaford. Weekends of tennis and night tennis under the heavy old lights working off a generator. No electricity, of course. They often held American tournaments. I'm not sure what an American tournament was, it just sounded cool. In fact, it was probably some kind of event that the Americans call a round robin. Even though the Brits owned Wimbledon the tennis Mecca, the Americans had all the best players. The wooden rackets had little pictures of these champions on the racket throat pieces. There was "Richard" Pancho Gonzales on the Spalding and Jack Kramer on the Wilson, both brands from the USA.

I think the Aussie stars came along later. We had Frank Sedgman who won Wimbledon when I was one, still in nappies. Later on Rod Laver and Ken Rosewall were featured on the Dunlop and Slazenger rackets. I became so hooked on tennis even though cricket was still in the picture that my Dad built me a practice wall. I think my parents were tired of me hitting against the narrow little outhouse a.k.a. the dunny or thunder box. This would leave dirty brown marks on the wall and wear out what little lawn or grass we had. Dad erected a backboard, levelled the ground a bit, then I would whack balls against the board for hours after school. My budding tennis career very nearly never started because one day I was bitten twice on the bum by a redback spider, right there in the dunny. Redback bites can be very serious, if not lethal, but I must have been bitten by the male spider (the female is the dangerous one, naturally enough) and I did not need a doctor. Making the 25 mile trip to Tara would have been fruitless anyway because a poisonous bite would have killed me by the time we reached a doctor or hospital. Nevertheless, I survived, missed a day or two of school and continued to pound away on the wall.

My memory is a bit hazy about my tennis in Hannaford in the early days. I had two tennis buddies, Greg and Darcy. My very first tournament, I recall, was in a little crappy place called Cabawin. And I did win big time, cleaned up in three events: two singles and a doubles (surely it was not a mixed doubles trophy because I did not know any girls then). I was so ecstatic. Three trophies, little cups literally the size of eggcups engraved with my name and my partner's. It was a little like winning Wimbledon except I did not know about the big "W" yet.

I collected quite a few eggcups over the next few years but looking back the draws must have been a little thin. Perhaps me, Darcy, Greg and a few more hackers, but hey there was nothing like a Win next to your name, even if it's a Win over your grandmother.

School was fun but weird. Imagine a single room, one teacher and all the grades, one through seven, in the room? Nice and tight, but there were only about 25 kids in all. My mum packed me off to school when I had just turned four. Got me out of the house early, I guess. My brother and I would ride our homemade bikes around five miles along the dirt road, stash our bikes, then get picked up by a bus (Darcy's Dad had the school run) for the remaining two miles to Hannaford State School. Invariably my bike did not go so well—it was a lemon—so Phillip doubled me on his bike or, so they tell me, I sometimes jogged the five miles each way. That may have prepared me for these long clay court matches years later in Europe. I knew there was a plan in place.

We had some interesting teachers in the bush. One stands out more vividly than the others. He was a young teacher, 21, fresh out of teacher's college in Brisbane and totally obsessed with 'roo shooting. A real city slicker. Some slow hot afternoons, he would fetch his .22 rifle from the back room and then we would all crowd around him as he took pot shots out the classroom windows at random crows. We loved it. And the afternoons would go much faster. For some unknown reason the P&C committee did not approve. He did not last too long as our teacher. Can't understand why.

I can well imagine though how a young teacher was excited about shooting and hunting. To me it was a huge adrenaline rush too. I loved going up the bush with my Dad and he would always take the rifle, an automatic .22 in case we came across some wild boar. The feral pigs were a real menace to our sheep. In lambing season these monster pigs would savage the ewes as they gave birth and take the newborn lambs. Even the weakened mothers would be vulnerable. Very sad, not to mention the devastation to the sheep population.

My thrill of thrills was when I had the OK to go off shooting alone. Well, with our dog, too. Off we would trek with the trusty weapon and a pocket full of ammo. I never did shoot much. The target was wild boar. The kangaroos (too cute to shoot) were sort of off limits because they were not really a pest to the graziers even though they could eat a lot of precious sheep feed. 'Roos were more of a pest to the crop farmers. To a ten-year old boy this was the ultimate thrill and adventure with just me and the dog and 5,000 acres of semi bush country to explore. That thrill and excitement must be like winning Wimbledon. Not that I even was close to doing that. But winning a big tennis match or even the whole tennis tournament never replicated the adrenaline buzz of "going shooting."

My Dad had a couple of pastimes, or pursuits if you will, that gave him his buzz. His sport was wood chopping. He was an accomplished axeman, a woodchopper, and he would venture off to compete in country shows, some many miles away from home. The wood chopping events were real fun to watch and were extremely popular at these shows. A little scary when you are flailing away with a five-pound axe as sharp as a razor. But my Dad was good—he never lost any toes or feet. This sport is one of the most physical sports you could wish to take on. And the guys won cash prizes in those days. They were way ahead of tennis players, the poor amateurs who only won eggcups.

The blue ribbon axe event in these competitions was the tree-felling event. Now this was just crazy. My Dad did not do this one (those dodgy knees again).

In the tree felling event the axeman had to scale a pole, much like a telegraph pole, then cut into two a big block that was nailed to the top. This entailed making your way up one side of the pole in stages using springboards—long boards with a tongue of steel in the end—cutting half the block, then scurrying down to climb up the other side. First man to sever the block won. I would not like to be up there about ten metres off the ground, swaying around on the board, hoping each time you swung the five pound axe your little piece of steel would hold up. That is a long fall with a razor sharp axe following your descent.

My wood chopping exploits were contained to swinging an axe around the neighbourhood of our house. After three incidents I remember where I chopped into my foot with a semi sharp axe (not my dad's weapons, fortunately), I decided not to go pro. Those little canvas sandshoes did not do much to protect the toes. I remember a lot of blood. And I still carry some scars to this day.

My dad's other pastime was collecting snakes, namely the death adder. Yes, healthy, fat, alive death adders. They are ranked number two or three most deadly snake on the planet (Australia has nine of the top ten most venomous snakes). Why did he do this nonsense? Well, maybe breaking in wild horses, buckjumping, and wood chopping was not enough excitement for him. Actually, he made a little cash on the side. The adders were sent off to a snake farm near Brisbane to be milked for their anti-venom. This was then used as an antidote for snakebite victims.

It is quite lucky no one in our family was ever bitten. After all, my brother, three sisters, and me were all running around barefoot most of the time. Once the old snake guru, Harry Honkey, from Brisbane came out to our place for a weekend to look for certain varieties of lizards and snakes. He reckoned there would be roughly 300 snakes of various kinds within a 250-yard radius of our house. A sobering thought. He was a fearless old bugger and had been bitten by numerous snakes including the death adder. He was pretty much immune to every bite by this time.

We had all varieties, the dangerous eastern brown, red-bellied black, copper heads, death adders, tree snakes to name some. My

Dad would have to handle the adders by hand (very carefully) then cage them up until he had collected a few. They were then sent off on the train to Brisbane packaged "handle with care" and "fragile" printed on the boxes.

My close call with an adder came when I was about three years old. I had somehow noticed a snake asleep under the dunny, the same dunny where I was to hit many a tennis ball later. I was eyeball to eyeball with this guy who was asleep, luckily, but I was trying to poke him with a stick to awaken him. Fortunately someone yanked me out before I pissed the adder off. Lucky for me, because they tend to strike like lightning and then you're very dead. Hence the name death adder. The hospital in Tara would have been no use because you have only a few minutes before the poison takes affect. I survived a match point against me that day.

Soon it was time to leave the bush.

An option was high school in nearby Tara. My parents discussed that option, but not for long. We, or they, rather, decided it was better for me to go a bit further afield to the big city, Toowoomba. It seemed like a logical choice to go there for some better competition in cricket and tennis and perhaps to get some coaching for the first time. That made sense but the only downside was I had to board in Toowoomba. I was going to a State School rather than a boarding school. The private schools had a good name, as they do today, but it does cost a bit to attend those schools. I ended up boarding with an elderly couple who were a little on the eccentric side. I think it was somewhat traumatic for a naïve twelve-year old bush kid coming to the "big smoke" for the first time.

A number of Australia's name tennis players spent their humble beginnings in the country areas, some quite remote, before venturing to the big city to further their tennis ambitions. In Queensland, we had Rod Laver (the Rockhampton "Rocket", although Rocky is a small coastal town), Mal Anderson (from Theodore), Pat Rafter (from Mt. Isa), and Roy Emerson (from Blackbutt). In New South

Wales, country stars were Margaret Court (Albury), Tony Roche (Tarcutta), and Evonne Goolagong (Barellan). South Australia had John Fitzgerald (Cockaleechie). Yes there is a place somewhere out there with that name. There were many others, maybe not future stars like those players, but they all sought the city life for that all important stronger competition. Roy Emerson ("Emmo") would delight in telling the tennis reporters in America where he was from. Americans usually think every Aussie comes from Sydney or "Mel-Born" and occasionally they may have heard of "Bris-bane". Never Toowoomba though. So Emmo would love saying his hometown was Blackbutt (so named after the black trunks of local trees). I'm sure they must have thought he was pulling their legs.

I wasn't a star player but I came from the country with that same plan to further my sporting skills. At the same time my doubles partner, Ross Case, came into Toowoomba from a dairy farm his folks owned about half an hour out of the city. We spent many hours practicing together and became a pretty good doubles team in the local and State tournaments. Often we would fight it out for the singles titles and the age division and junior championships.

Luckily for me I had my older brother to keep an eye on me in those early high school days. He is four years older and had preceded me at the same school. We played tennis at the same clubs but he probably used to playing with his peers more than with me. Phillip was a good player and won the Toowoomba City Championships one time.

I had some private tennis lessons for a while with the local pro, Perc Gaydon. Perc was a good, positive influence. In his day he had represented Queensland in the interstate competition and had two brothers who were also very good players at the local and State level.

My cricket at high school and at club level was all going well too. But it was taking up my weekends and clashing with the tennis tournaments, which were usually held on the weekends in surrounding areas. I was one of our star batsmen and someone my team relied upon to score some runs. In two of my first games I had scored 100, which is quite difficult to do in the timeframe of an afternoon game. My high school coach was getting a little peeved with me begging off weekends in succession to go off to the country tennis tournaments. Ultimately I committed to one of the playoff games on a Saturday but then I remembered my eldest sister Lynne was getting married that day. I was too scared to renege on my coach once again so I skipped my sister's wedding to play my school match. Probably not the best decision but I just did not have the heart to bag on them again. Sorry, Lynne, and thanks for making it to my wedding years later in Kauai, Hawaii.

So it was time to make a decision. Tennis, or cricket? In my senior year I chose to go the tennis route. I think it was the right decision to chase the individual sport rather than the team sport. Only twelve guys play on a selected cricket team. That's a big "if" as to whether you make the team to represent your city, State or eventually your Country. What if the selectors did not like you? Tennis on the other hand is individualistic—you are on your own, only you can do it. I liked that concept more.

During my senior year and close to final exams my maths teacher, Mr Grunke, would give me a hard time if I did not turn my assignments in on a Monday morning. This was often the case after a weekend tennis tournament. I was a little scared of Mr Grunke because he could throw a blackboard duster at your face or twist your ear until you cried out. One Monday morning he nailed me in front of class. "Playing tennis," he snorted: "this fellow was playing tennis instead of doing his maths homework. Fellow (everyone was called" fellow" he never used first names) ,do you honestly think you will be a tennis player? How about university?" "Yes sir, that's sort of the plan, tennis for a living" "Well good luck making a living, fellow" he replied sarcastically.

About 13 years later I happened to be back in Toowoomba for a little R&R. it turned out to be my High School's 25-year anniversary. I went along curious to catch up with some old classmates. Walking around the campus I chanced upon Mr Grunke. He recognised me and amazingly came up and shook my hand. "I owe you an apology fellow. I remember embarrassing you in front of the class one day in your senior year. You did chase your dream like you said. I've been following your progress in the papers. Well done, fellow". Mr Grunke was a nice old bastard after all. That was quite a noble gesture on his part.

My parents moved to Toowoomba sometime around my junior year. They had had enough of the sheep business. The weather is too fickle out there, either feast or famine. Some years too dry, some years too wet. Wool prices fluctuated and eventually the wool industry died somewhat so they sold the property.

I never did go back to the bush. Looking back, it toughened me up growing up out there. Conditions were a little basic: no electricity, no sewerage, no paved roads and not much fresh food to eat. Not even any television, video games, or mobile phones, amazingly. I think kids tend to grow up well in that environment and learn some life lessons.

My folks started an art gallery on the edge of Toowoomba. That was quite a change from grazing sheep: a total 180-degree turn. My Dad built the gallery; an unusual decagon design and they sold art works produced by many artists from all over the country. Mum did her painting as well as teaching art. Dad turned his hand to sculpture and later on did some commissioned works for many towns and stud farms around the country. He mainly did horses or bulls, usually cast in bronze. Also his leatherwork is featured in the Stockmen's Hall of Fame in Longreach. Quite a legacy he left. The gallery eventually became the biggest provincial gallery in Australia. Talented parents, so where did I go wrong?

Ross and I were doing well in the junior tournaments and even were competitive in the Open Men's events. We had done a couple of forays down to Sydney and tried our hand with the best junior players in the country. Along with our friend, Geoff Masters, we had some great results against the Sydney stars.

It was time to move further afield then Toowoomba. We committed to Brisbane on weekends to get some better and stronger matches. The summer of 1967 we found work as runners for the pros during the Davis Cup Challenge Round, the final as it was known in those days. The defending Nation was in the final without going through any preliminary matches throughout the year. This time the defending champion country, Australia, was up against Spain on the grass courts of Milton Stadium in Brisbane. This was the first big match I had witnessed. The Aussie stars John Newcombe (then the current Wimbledon champion in 1967) and Roy Emerson (already a double Wimbledon champion) were battling the legendary Manolo Santana (the 1966 Wimbledon champion) and the rising world star, Manuel Orantes. What an awesome final. Australia prevailed 4-1 after Santana, the genius on any surface, had upset Newc in the opening match. Sure, I wanted to be like these guys, they really impressed me.

Little did we know a few weeks later Ross and I would be facing Orantes and his doubles partner team mate in Davis Cup, Juan Gisbert, in the quarter finals of the Australian Championships on the grass at Kooyong, Melbourne. Amazingly we had won through three rounds in the Open doubles draw. Pretty heady stuff for two Toowoomba schoolboys. Then in the quarter-finals we had Orantes-Gisbert two sets to love on the grass. We ended up losing in five sets. I think our mistake was to take the optional break after the third set. Too much time to consider our situation: we're beating the Spanish Davis Cup stars on one of the biggest stages. The semi-finals of a Grand Slam? Wow, too much. Imagine how McEnroe felt as a 17 year old, in his first appearance at Wimbledon and in the semi-finals? Knowing him, he was probably pissed off he did not win the whole thing first go at it.

Anyway it was exciting for two 16 year olds at their first Aussie Open.

The next year I moved to Brisbane and worked in a sporting goods company. One of their lines was Spalding tennis equipment. They sponsored me with my gear and gave me lots of time off to practice and train. I did not have a coach, after leaving Mr Gaydon behind in Toowoomba, and I think that was a mistake not to have someone guiding me to the next level. It was a little mysterious how to make that transition from the junior competition to the open level with the big boys. Soon I would be heading out onto the world stage and honestly I was a little lost, not knowing what was required to get there.

Ross and I had been selected for the Junior Davis Cup squad, the elite squad in Australia for juniors. The legendary Harry Hopman was the Davis Cup captain and he had seemingly won a million Cups for Australia with his superstar cast of players over the years. He was our coach, too, but we never saw him. Soon he was to jump ship and head to America to start his own Academy. "Hop" I learned later was a pretty ruthless little man, a fantastic motivator and trainer, but he played favourites and did not care who he stomped on. Pity, we never really had the chance to work under him. I would have loved the physical discipline under Hoppy.

So I spent my time in Brisbane as a storeman, a shit kicker if you will, but I had lots of time to practice and my employer paid my wage (albeit a lowly one) to compete during the summer season in the State championships around Australia on the grass courts of Sydney, Melbourne, Adelaide, Hobart, and our own Brisbane. Ross was doing a similar version of the shit kicker with his sponsor, Slazenger, also in Brisbane.

Then in early 1969 the journey was about to begin for me.

Chapter 6

Across the Channel

After Wimbledon everyone seemed to go off to many different places and tournaments. It felt like a bit of a downer after Wimbledon, an anti-climax. This was the pinnacle of the year. Now it was time for the second chapter.

Some of the top players would take time off after Wimbledon. A little R&R after those punishing matches in Paris followed by the fortnight of another Grand Slam a few weeks later at Wimbledon. However it did not appear to worry Bjorn Borg who won the French-Wimbledon double four times. And in current times Rafa Nadal is doing more than OK on the grass after his" gimmie "title at the French Open. Traditionally you would not see the big boys for some time after Wimbledon was done.

There were quite a few options for tournaments come the beginning of July. Some guys did the US summer circuit starting at Newport, Rhode Island, the last remaining grass tournament in the USA, then on to the very hot, humid tournaments of Washington (DC), Indianapolis (IND), Louisville (KY), Cincinnati (Oh), Chicago (Ill), Atlanta (GA), South Orange (New Jersey), Stowe (Vermont), North Conway (New Hampshire), cumulating in the US Open at New York. The Open was played at Forest Hills out on Long Island (grass surface) and later moved to the public facility at Flushing Meadows (hard court surface), also on Long Island.

Across the channel on the Continent there were literally hundreds of tournaments to choose from. Besides the National

Champs in Switzerland (Gstaad), Holland (Hilversum), Sweden (Båstad), Austria (Kitzbuhel), and others, there were countless little events all over France, Spain, Italy, Austria, Germany and the other European countries. If you were adventurous you could find some tournaments down in Yugoslavia, Czechoslovakia, and in some other Eastern bloc places all summer long.

I remember one of the South African players, Croise Van der Merve, a nice dude with quite a thick Afrikaans accent, asked me when I was going across the "kennel" after Wimbledon. I had no clue what he was talking about for a while. Something to do with dogs maybe? Then he mentioned the "fairies" and it clicked. Of course, the ferry across the Channel! Often we would take the ferry across the English Channel, usually from Dover or Folkestone to the ports in Normandy, usually Calais or Boulogne, before making our assault on the Continental tournaments. This was Croise's first time across the "kennel". I think he needed some advice on how to catch the "fairies" or someone to hold his hand.

The Brits would talk about going abroad or going on the continent. I don't think they considered themselves part of Europe, this small island off the coast of Europe, separated by a "kennel". That may have changed now that Britain is a member of the EEC and the euro is the currency, not the British pound.

Some of my best memories in England were of playing a handful of the summer tournaments on grass after Wimbledon. The tournaments were mainly held in the northern parts of England, the weather was usually nice in July and the atmosphere was very laid back.

In my first year overseas I did a few weeks in England before heading off to the clay again. One of my favourite tournaments was in Felixstowe, a small town on the North Sea coast in Suffolk. The hospitality was amazing. Quite a few of the Aussies and American players were housed with a Mr John Cobbold who owned Tolly Cobbold Breweries. John was an eccentric bachelor who lived in a veritable mansion on the outskirts of Felixstowe. What a great place to stay for a week, a mansion to ourselves while Mr Cobbold would take us out to one of his hotels or restaurants each night. He was very entertaining and threw a magnificent bash on the finals night of the tournament. We also played some tennis that week. It was great playing grass court tournaments because play would not commence until 10 or 11am—by this time the hangover was gone—and play could continue until 9pm in the twilight, although that late finish might cut into one's social life.

Felixstowe was one of my first tournament wins in England. So I had good memories. The winner's cheque of £35, yes that's correct, £35 (about $70) did not go too far. But who cared, it was an awesome week and a "W" next to my name.

Another great hospitable tournament was in Hoylake. It's also a seaside town, up in Merseyside on the other side of the England coast. Hoylake had a great sponsorship, one of the cigarette companies, and the prize money was quite decent and totally against the nature of these events. Another decent aspect was the "hospitality" girls who were working the tournament for the cigarette company. Often the British Open golf was going on in July and sometimes not too far away. Depending on the rotation, it was held at nearby Royal Lytham St. Anne's or Royal Hoylake. Sometimes the Aussie golfers visited us but I don't think they cared about our tennis. They were chasing the cute girls who did the Open as well. To his credit one of Australia's great golf stars ended up marrying one of these girls who was in Hoylake employed by the cigarette company.

OK. Enough of jolly old England. Time to go off hacking around on the red dirt of the Continent. No more bacon and eggs for breakfast or tea and scones for a while. Bring on the croissants, chocolat chaud and sandwich de jambon, my staples in France. Another thing we were going to miss was the laundromats in England. So easy to find a laundrette there and so convenient. But over on the

Continent it was the drudgery of washing out the red dust, which really stained your tennis socks, in the shower or in the bathroom washbasin. Usually it was too expensive to send your laundry out in the hotels. Remember we were the paupers of the tennis circuit. Some players simply walked into the showers and washed out the red dust still wearing their gear.

Along with "Digger" Hammond, my travel buddy /doubles partner, we set off that first year to play predominately throughout France and Spain. We were reliant on those replies from tournament directors who would hopefully offer full hospitality and maybe a few dollars. So we could not be too picky—it was just a matter of taking an offer wherever it came from. A lot of tournaments would not even reply. But it was great when a tournament did respond with a little deal. The $100 guarantee and hospitality was a good standard. I did snag some good deals, occasionally. Once I was offered $300 and air ticket from Paris to Casablanca and similarly an invitation to play in Beirut with air travel from London. We did make some boo-boos however. For example, one of the earlier tournaments to accept us was a small one in the very north of Denmark. Well, Europe is a small continent, right? That was fine but our next one was down in the top part of Spain. We had flown to Copenhagen but the logistics of getting to Bilbao (or near San Sebastian) was quite ridiculous. Our mode of transport was train, which was quite effective in say, France, but in Spain it was pretty much a slow moving cattle train.

The French tournaments were a bit easy to organise. We could call the French Federation de Tennis in Paris and they would set up a tournament for us. Or you could call directly. That was not easy in my broken French. The French would give all foreign players an assimilated ranking. Everyone who played tennis in France would have a ranking under the National System, whether you were a complete hacker (non classé) all the way up to the elite first series classement. Those players who had competed in the French

Open, for example, were more likely to be assimilated as first series (the top 15 players) or the top of the second series. That was a good system because the better players only showed up later in the week to play the tableau final, the final draw. And if you were really smart, you could almost juggle two tournaments in the same week. Say, play a little week-long tournament in Holland, pick up your guarantee (probably not much prize money involved anyway), conveniently lose your match there by Thursday, then hop on the train to somewhere in France for that tableau final tournois commencing on Friday. Easy.

We played dozens of tournaments around Normandy and down the coast of France all the way to the Spanish border. One tournament stood out that first summer was in the resort town of Deauville in Normandy. This quaint town was like a summer playground for the rich and famous, the horse racing was well known to Deauville, as was the Casino. We were put up at the Hotel Royal, a very fancy establishment and, even better, all our accommodation and meals were free. One semi-permanent resident of the hotel was the famous actor, Omar Sharif of Dr Zhivago fame. Apparently Omar was one of the best bridge players in the world and the world tournament was going on at the adjacent Casino that July. The only down side to our hospitality was you were required to wear a coat and tie in the dining room. Not having any dressy clothes in our suitcases, just lots of tennis kit and jeans, we had to borrow a jacket and tie. Failing that, you had to take your dinner in the kitchen with the staff. No bending the house rules. It was a good week and fun to rub shoulders with our" buddy" Omar.

In the Deauville tournament "Digger" was completely devastated because he had lost to a young lefty two weeks in a row. I did not see either match but apparently "Digger" would come to the net on this kid's backhand and the boy passed him about 800 times (it seemed), mainly down the line. I was not great with condolences. I said something like "Aw, shit happens mate. Maybe next time you play him try his forehand a bit more or cover the line a little more on that backhand pass," And "you are going to throw in some dodgy losses from time to time". I think "Digger" took it hard because the kid was so young, just 16, and he was travelling with his Mum from Argentina, to boot.

As it turned out this kid, Guillermo Vilas, was pretty "useful", particularly on clay. He won a French Open (as well as making three finals there), the US Open (when it was played on har tru clay) and back-to-back Australian Opens (on Kooyong grass). He became number one in the world in 1977 and his 46-match winning streak that summer is still a record. He won 53 consecutive matches on clay that year starting in Paris (Borg did not play that year, luckily for Vilas) and cumulated in the US Open win over Jimmy Connors. Sorry "Digger" it wasn't such a bad loss after all, it just seemed so at the time mate.

A little more on Vilas: I played him during his monumental year of 1977. We met in the Austrian Championships, which were held on clay in Kitzbuhel, up in the Alps of the Tyrol. This was a couple of weeks after Wimbledon and I was playing pretty well and I enjoyed the faster conditions in the altitude. Vilas was a bit dodgy after bombing out early in Wimbledon. He had won the French Open a few weeks earlier but the soft grass and low bounce of the Wimbledon grass did not favour his heavy topspin game. He had great success on the higher bouncing Australian Open grass at Kooyong, winning twice there as well as at the World Masters also at Kooyong. So he came to Kitzbuhel a bit rusty and probably lacking in confidence although this was his surface, clay. This guy spent a lot of time on the practice courts. It was not unusual for him to hit for four or five hours before his match. That seemed crazy but he was amazingly fit and strong. Perhaps he learned that regimen from another lefty, Rod Laver, who also lived on the practice courts.

In our first round match (I had won through three qualifying matches) I led 5-2 and served for the set. Vilas seemed very nervous and very shaky. He did not enjoy my low flat forehands and sliced, shortish backhands. His great coach/mentor/manager, Ion Tiriac, was sitting in the front row behind the court looking ever menacing and chain smoking as usual. Tiriac was the man who moulded the greats like Nastase, Vilas and Becker, making them into super stars and making himself an obscene amount of money at the same time. The Romanian was talking to his charge constantly in one of his seven languages, probably Italian or Spanish, telling Vilas to slow the game down and take a huge amount of time between points. Where was the Grand Prix supervisor? There is a no coaching rule in tennis and also a rule of 25 seconds between points. But in 1977 I'm not sure if these rules were viable yet.

I started to think about the situation, 5-2 and serving. This guy was very beatable that day. But unfortunately I tightened (some people may say I choked) and ended up blowing that set. Then I lost the match. Good coaching "Tiri". He always was a smart player himself when he was one of the best players in all of Europe and part of the all-time best doubles team of Nastase—Tiriac. One of his great moves, I think, was in 1984 when he was coaching Boris Becker. He just knew this 17 year old was the next super star. At Wimbledon that year Boris sprained his ankle in his second round match against the American, Tim Mayotte, a great player on grass. This was deep in the match, the fourth set I recall, and Boris came up to offer his hand to Mayotte. Match over, default time. But Tiriac was acutely aware of the newly introduced injury time out rule. He yelled out to Boris (probably in German this time) not to shake hands yet, but to call for the trainer. Three minutes time out plus treatment was allowed. The rest is history: Boris hung on after taping his ankle, won in five sets, then went on to win Wimbledon over Kevin Curran in the final. Amazing. The most amazing tennis result ever, his debut Wimbledon win, in my opinion.

After my match with Vilas he seemed to get better every match in Kitzbuhel winning the tournament, then winning everything on the way to Forest Hills with his memorable US Open win over Connors in the final. He even won after the US Open in the Paris event until his streak ended at Aix-en-Provence in the south of France. He defaulted the final to Nastase in protest when "Nasty" used the crazy spaghetti-strung racquet, which was banned soon after.

Here I was starting Vilas off on his 46 match-winning streak. The record stands to this day. Earlier in Paris that year I had started the young McEnroe out on his first Grand Slam singles match win. Something about beating Gardiner, the Aussie Journeyman, really inspired those guys! A win over him, confidence exploded, and those guys were almost invincible.

Meanwhile we were back in the land of the French. These were such wonderful little resort towns where we played, coastal places like La Baule, Royan, Arcachon, Bayonne, Biarritz and other quaint little towns scattered around the interior. The hospitality was always great. Such great food and wine. Pity I was not a wine drinker in those days. I remember playing little tournaments in Cognac and Champagne. You can imagine the gifts we received in the bottle form. Truly wasted on us.

Another tournament that stood out in my memory that summer of 1969 was at Aix-en-Provence. A small town in the Midi and amazingly hot in July. I recall one night sitting outside our hotel because it was so hot even at night. Everyone seemed to be inside watching TV, nobody was outside. Unbeknownst to "Digger" and me the French people were watching a couple of Americans walking on the moon. We had missed the Neil and Buzz show. I was so disappointed. I read about it later in the International Herald Tribune, my only link with the outside world then.

One memory of Aix-en-Provence was to see the legendary man from Blackbutt, Roy Emerson win the singles. "Emmo" was such a legend in France. He was a double French Open winner in singles besides winning the doubles in Paris from 1960 to1965. That's six straight titles with five different Aussie partners! Something I did not know then was Emmo has won the singles and doubles in all four Grand Slam events. Unparalleled today.

In Aix 1969, Emmo was over 30 years of age and still as fit as a Mallee bull. He won the final there in a trot. What an athlete. One afternoon, we were having lunch out on the terrace at the Country Club next to Emmo and his friends. I did not think he knew these two Aussie juniors sitting there. He came over to me with his typical smile and said, "How 'ya going Blue?" (Anyone and everyone he called "Blue"). "Hope the frogs are treating you good". My hero and he acknowledged us. Probably one of the fittest men on the planet then I'm sure, and one of the friendliest, outgoing champions.

One of our big mistakes in those days was the train travel. We went through tremendous "aggro" to get around by train. Trains are very good in Europe, particularly in France but when you have so much stuff to carry, it was tough. And taxis were a bit out of our budget. We left Australia on a six or seven month long journey with ten or twelve wooden racquets, a suitcase full of tennis gear including about 50 sets of natural gut tennis strings and a bag full of shoes. These racquets had to last the whole tour even though we may have picked up some extra frames in London. Most of the players were with Dunlop in London or Slazenger where the parent company was down in Surrey, England. I don't know when some smart guy invented the little wheels on suitcases and retractable handles to pull them along? Wish I had that patent. It would have made life so much easier back then, rather than lugging those heavy bags everywhere. I'm sure my chronic neck and back problems originated from all those days of carrying a heavy lopsided load from train stations to hotels.

We seemed to have quite a few faux pas in our first year, the learning year, for "Digger" and me. One screw up was on a French train. We were heading east to a little place somewhere near Chamonix in the French Alps. These French trains were much quicker than the cattle trains of backward old Spain and southern Italy. Invariably these were crammed with smelly peasants, carrying everything from chickens, goats and wine. We thought they were weird; imagine how they stared when the blue-eyed aliens would struggle into the compartment with dozens of tennis racquets and way too much luggage? On our way to Chamonix our train did not appear to stop at our station. Soon we were passing though the Douane (customs) into Switzerland on our way to Geneva. We were on the express train. Uh oh, we had overshot by one country. No worries, every place is fairly close in Europe and we did get back to France after a 20-minute stay in Switzerland then a retreat back over the border.

The Italian

Another gaffe came the next week. We were heading down to Milano, Italy for the world under 21 tournament. This was a great tournament to be invited to and pretty much the last stop before flying home to Australia in September. "Digger" and I had met up with another Aussie duo, Syd Ball ("Side Agate") and Bob Giltinan ("Gilto"), doubles partners from Sydney. We were traveling from Switzerland and it was necessary to change trains in Locarno to catch the southbound train to Milano. As luck would have it we pulled into the station and our Milano train was already sitting on the adjacent track right next to us. Someone in our group had the bright idea of just transferring all our gear through the open window of our train into the other train rather than lug all this stuff up the stairs and around to the other platform. What a perfect plan. Two guys scurried around to the Milano train and the remaining two stayed behind and passed all those bags and racquets though the windows to them. In the midst of this manoeuvre both trains started to move off in opposite directions. We knew two guys were heading to Milano with some of their own gear and while the other two guys were off to who knows where with some of their own gear (maybe). It all worked out eventually, all four of us ended up in Milano and we were reunited with our own stuff. Just another day in the life of the tennis traveller.

Milano was a good week to let the hair down. It was the last stop before going home to Australia after a long six or seven months overseas. We decided to hit the boulevards of Milano. Four of us piled in a taxi and out we went looking for the professional girls. "Gilto" and his fellow Davis Cupper, who I will call by his nickname "Nugget" to protect his identity, were seasoned pros. They had travelled the previous year to Europe in the official touring team under the strict fox, Mr Hopman. This was to be the last touring team under the "Hop" before he left Australia for greener pasture in the States. Anyway "Gilto " and "Nugget" had been around the block and were good street wise guys to be around.

Our cabbie took us along this long boulevard where the girls worked. The only problem was the Italian hotels did not allow guests to come to your hotel room. There were very strict house rules on this kind of action.

The taxi driver negotiated with two girls on behalf of "Nugget" and me. The other two guys decided to go on foot then get another taxi. We understand the negotiated price, ocho mille lire (8,000 lire), a mere $US5 each in 1969 money. An extraordinary deal: cheap at half the price.

We somehow communicated to the girls that we had no apartment or house and they knew the hotel was not an option. They had a solution, however. Our cabbie dropped us down the road on the corner. "Nugget" and I were a little bewildered because there was only a petrol station here. What was going on? "No comprendo". With much gesturing from the Italians we realised the "Servo" was the place, right next to the petrol pumps. You cannot be serious. This is my first adventure and we are out in the open at a petrol station? Well, what can you expect for five bucks?

Luckily there were no patrons in the petrol station this late at night. I did not mind "Nugget" was about nine inches away from me but it was a little unnerving seeing some faces at the windows of the adjacent high-rise apartment. It was typical of a tennis match in Italy. Lots of noise and abuse from the spectators just like playing against an Italian at Foro Italico. Luckily this match was short. I was embarrassed and glad it was over.

"Nugget" and I became legendary for a while in the tennis fraternity. We were dubbed the petrol pump boys, the" bowser brothers" of Milano.

We did get to play some tennis in Milano, too. The best young players from Europe (and Australia) were invited to the Tennis Club Milano. I remember seeing the young future stars, like Ivan Lendl and Adriano Panatta, the Italian superstar and a skinny little girl from Czechoslovakia, Martina Navratilova, on her first time out from behind the Iron Curtain.

Also in Milano I was to get my first groupie. She was an older girl/lady (30 something) from Belgium. Her name was Francoise (mais naturellement) and she loved Aussie players in particular. She had fallen for "Gilto " and "Nugget" the previous year and now she zeroed in on me. I did not mind, she was quite nice, very polite with her limited English, but she ended up following me around Europe for the next eight years. Now that's a bit weird.

I never would converse with her but she would write letters care of my racquet company, Slazenger, in London. She would give me lots of photos of my matches along with the local newspaper cuttings. I do not know how she knew my itinerary but Francoise would simply show up at my tournaments. I would go out for a match in Barecolona, Montana (in Switzerland), Terracina (Italy), or even Wimbledon on court twelve and there she would be, the lone spectator in the stands long before the match took to court. Then after a few photos, a note would be pressed in my hand, then "au revoir". A few weeks later (I did not even know where I was playing three weeks out) she would reappear.Once Francoise tracked me down at my parents place in Toowoomba—she obtained the address from the Belgian Embassy in Canberra. Maybe she was working with the CIA. A lovely lady but it was eerie sometimes.

I really enjoyed playing in Rome, the Eternal City. Not that I played the Italian Championships much, maybe a few times over the years. The Foro Italico was such a spectacular setting, the centre court with the big marble statues surrounding the stadium. A left over from the 1960 Olympic Games. The outside courts, pairs of sunken red clay courts were set amongst a grove of lovely elegant cypress trees making it quite an idyllic setting. You could watch a match from the terrace, have a cappuccino and five courses of pasta, take a siesta, come back and the game would still be going on. The matches involving an Italian versus a foreigner were extraordinary, loud and theatrical. Lots of drama, a bit of parochial assistance, naturally enough, by the local linesmen and umpires for their favourite sons. One year the great Bjorn Borg played the Italian Open for his first time. He won the tournament—it was on clay—but he received such extraordinary abuse after beating his Italian opponent in the final. Bad line calls, verbal abuse, coin throwing (a popular one). He vowed never to play the Italian again. True to his word he didn't come back.

One of my favourite stories about the Italian involved their National Champs played on that same stadium court. In the final Fausto Gardini (no relation), their National champion back then, beat one of his other big rivals. Well he did not beat the other guy, the umpire (probably in Gardini's pay) had made an unbelievable overrule which ended up winning the match for Gardini. In the pandemonium and subsequent calling for the referee and chaos in the crowd, Gardini quickly wound the net down picked up his gear and the net and was out of there. He took the net with him figuring there would be no way they could replay that point now. Match over. What a great play. There is nothing in the tennis rulebook about taking the net away. In Rome 1978 I met Vilas again. He was with the wily Ion Tiriac who was one of the best doubles players of the era, especially when he was partnered with his countryman Ilie Nastase. "Tiri" was not a natural player but very cagey. He looked like count Dracula, a scary looking guy with a droopy moustache. He would look you right in the eye and say "Don't break my balls" and watch out for his head butt. A guy who chews up pint beer mugs and spits out the pieces of glass (his party trick) is a tough dude I guess.

They were the number one seeds in Rome that year. Vilas was the number one seed in singles, and the current number one player in the world at that time.

My first time partner in Rome was Paul McNamee from Melbourne. We drew the number one seeds first round in the doubles. Shockingly the previous day, Vilas lost his first round match in singles (I can't recall who beat him) so "Macca" tells me we will probably get a default from Villas-Tiriac. He said that Vilas would be out of there, on the first plane to Paris to get ready for his French Open defence. There was no way he was going to stick around for the doubles even if it drew a fine from the ATP for withdrawal without a legitimate injury excuse.

Nevertheless, they did show up for the match. "Macca" was surprised but then he said these guys are going to do a tank job for sure (make like they are trying but lose the match on purpose). Definitely they will do a tank, mate. No question.

After we won the first set I was thinking maybe he's right. But when they won the second set and the match was all tied up deep in the final set I was a little dubious. "They are definitely tanking" Paul would say on the changeover. When the match extended to the third set tie-break, I said to Paul "Doesn't look like they're going to tank, mate. What you reckon?"

We squeaked out the tie-breaker, 7-5. If they tanked we had no inkling of it. Who tanks a match 7-6 in the third? Just lose 6-3, 6-3 and get the hell out of there. But knowing Tiriac he may have worked out the perfect tank job. "Macca" was such a good partner, quick as a flash and all over the net like a rash. He teamed up permanently with the other "Macca", Peter McNamara, also from Melbourne. They became a great team and snagged two Wimbledon doubles titles. How come my partners were ditching me, then they proceeded to win Wimbledon later on with someone else? First it was Ross Case and now Paul McNamee. I was getting a complex.

My last night in Rome that same year was very disturbing. I had returned to my hotel somewhere near the Vatican quite late after dinner as well as indulging in quite a few vino tintos. My room was on about the third floor of the pensione. I did not bother to close the window shutters, just slumped into bed. A potential burglar/robber after espying the open shutters, climbed up the side of the hotel somehow onto a little landing. At around 4am he climbed into my room window. Suddenly I woke up, grabbed my trusty aluminium Yonex racquet and ran at him ready for a forehand drive into his kneecaps. But he fled, was out the window and gone before I could execute. It was very scary at that hour of night. I decided to check out and head for the airport at 5am and get to a safer place, Paris.

Spain, The Dark Days

Some of the most traumatic weeks I have had on the road seemed to involve Spain. The trauma did not come during tennis matches (except for one which I would like to forget) but just with the travelling and off court stuff. Spain was a dark sort of place in those days, still under the regime of Generalissimo Franco. It had the atmosphere of a police State and it was quite a bit behind the times compared with the neighbouring European countries to the north.

In April 1972 I had headed down from London to play a few tournaments in the south of France on the Riviera. Probably not the smartest itinerary because it was difficult to get acceptance in these tournaments which had such small draws. At this time every man and his dog had emerged from the northern winter and wanted to get outdoors once again and play some tennis in the sun. So the French Riviera was the place to go. This was still pre ATP days and the ATP computerised rankings. Getting into these tournaments or even the qualifying draws for the tournament was certainly difficult and acceptance was reliant on a National ranking or previous record in France. But going to the Riviera was more romantic than staying in England and playing the minor circuit there in the cold and drizzle.

I had spent some time in London at our Aussie headquarters, Mrs Drake's B&B in Putney. Also, my brother Phil and wife Judy were spending a working holiday in London so I had a chance to hang out with them. Another dude from Sydney showed up at Mrs Drake's doorstep on his first tour to Europe. This guy, Allan Haswell, was a good young player who had already beaten a couple of the bigger names back in Australia. Alan was a very strong athletic person, very quick- tempered as I was to find out soon, and a good amateur boxer. As an amateur boxer in Sydney he had already won all his fights in the ring mostly by knockout.

Naturally enough Alan and I teamed up to travel across the channel and down to the south of France. We were going to play some doubles together whenever the opportunity arose. Alan was always gung-ho and ready to take on the world.

The big event on the Riviera was the Monte Carlo championships at the spectacular Monte Carlo country club. This was definitely the playground of the rich and famous. There were lead up tournaments in towns like Nice, Menton, and Beaulieu, but Monte Carlo was the big one. So big actually we did not get a game or even a chance to play the "Qualies". That was how tough the draw was and how limited the field. Our ranking status did not get us a look in. This was not one of those tournaments where you wrote a letter requesting hospitality and "x" dollars. No, you entered then showed up with hope of getting accepted. Monte Carlo was one of the world's elite tournaments. And it still is to this day one of the nine World Tour Masters 1000 events, the level below the four Slams.

It was the same scenario for the other poor buggers who showed up from Australia. These were three Queenslanders who I had known forever right through junior tennis ranks. They travelled as a team. Firstly, there was Greg Braun ("Blue") from Brisbane, "Blue" was just 18, on his first maiden tour and he was very green. His family had moved from a cattle property in central Queensland to the suburbs of the big city, Brisbane. Greg had led a very sheltered life so far; just cattle and tennis courts and he never strayed too far away from his beloved parents. This was his first taste of Europe and I don't think he was ready for Monte Carlo or the ensuing weeks in Spain. The second team member was Keith Hancock ("Kok"). "Kok" had moved to Queensland from a small coastal town, Casino, in New South Wales where his Dad managed a tick control gate. Guess they did not want those ticks heading north to Queensland. Keith was a fiery redhead with immense talent. He was amazingly quick around the court with an explosive game. When this country boy came to Brisbane people were comparing him with the other red headed boy from the bush, Rod Laver. They had similar ability and agility as youngsters (and similar complexions) but Rod was able to control the fire within perhaps a little better than Keith.

The dynamic duo was managed by Wayne Mason, another Brisbane-ite, who I had worked with at the Spalding racket company before my touring days had started. Wayne was a few years older than the other guys. His ambition was not to be a tennis pro per se, but to climb the ladder of the business world in the tennis industry. He had a great business sense and was a natural salesman. Wayne could sell ice cream to the eskimoes but he could piss them off too. Not a natural diplomat but he definitely knew his stuff around the tennis industry. Strangely enough he did not have a nickname as such, although he gave me mine, "Aggro", back at Spalding days

As it turned out Alan and I hung out with these three guys in Monte Carlo. We were all watching our pennies, or centimes in this case. Our digs in Monte Carlo was one big room over the courts, with five guys cramped in together. Our basic fare was baguettes and grand bouteilles de limonade. Not really healthy for athletes but it was cheap, which really mattered.

Monte Carlo was such a beautiful event. The multi-tiered levels of the red clay courts with the wonderful clubhouse and centre court were very picturesque. The Country Club overlooked the harbour and the azure blue Mediterranean, packed with millions of dollars' worth of spectacular yachts. Behind the country club rose the hills of Monaco and the quaint town: a picture postcard. The most famous Formula One motor race in the world is through those winding streets of Monte Carlo. A haven for the rich and famous besides being a tax haven for elite athletes

Pity we did not get to play some tennis in Monaco. But somehow we were invited to the wonderful players 'party held at the Casino de Monte Carlo. For a moment that night we felt like the rich and famous.

So Alan and I hitched a ride with Team Mason to the next stop, another big tournament, the torneo at the magnificent Club de Campo in Madrid. Wayne had purchased a small van in England during a previous circuit there. The van was painted with flowers, actually some herbs advertising a health elixir. So consequently it looked pretty much like a hippie mobile when we rolled up to the Spanish border at Irún late at night. The Spanish border police must have thought these guys were extremely dodgy looking foreigners. Five dishevelled, unshaven dudes climbing out of a van covered in marijuana like leaves. We were a bit beaten up after the journey from Monte Carlo, it was much farther than we had envisioned and we were cramped in that van along with 75 racquets and piles of luggage. Added to this two of the guys were still wearing party hats from the Monte Carlo soirée at the Casino. "Kok" wore his Aussie bush hat and must have looked like a real bushranger or even a Crocodile Dundee figure.

No surprise that the guards had hesitation in sending us back the way we had come, back to Francia. We dudes would not be entering the wonderful police state of Generalissimo Franco that night. Even if they understood any English these guys did not care that we had to be in Madrid tomorrow for our tennis tournament. And Madrid was still another 700 kilometres or so away.

Wayne and I, being the senior spokesmen of our group, approached the guard hut for the second time for a more diplomatic approach. We left our fellow hippies back in the van and went back to negotiate with those two guards armed with our letters from the Madrid Campo de Tennis. To no avail. These guards had had enough of the pushy foreigners and one guard, probably the dumber or drunker of the two, was really getting pissed off with us now. After getting no reaction from us after repeatedly saying "Francia"—we weren't budging until we were granted the right to enter Spain—he calmly unbuttoned his pistol holster, cocked the pistol and put it to my temple. And then likewise to Wayne's head. We could see some empty wine bottles on the floor. This was not the time to reason with an inebriated guy holding a gun to your head. I said: "You know, Wayne, he has a good point. We have not been to France for a while, what a grand idea".

Well, back to the drawing board. We had tennis matches the next day. But at least we did not get shot like a couple of tourists did sometime later in the 1970s at the same border. In retrospect I'm glad my friend Alan did not come with Wayne and me to negotiate. I'm sure he would have smashed those guys, gun or no gun.

OK, let's go to plan B. After consulting our rudimentary road map, I had the brilliant idea of backtracking a little, then circling around to the west somewhere and entering at another checkpoint, if in fact that existed miles away from Irún. There were little tiny red lines on the map that seemed to go into the Pyrénées Mountains then maybe through Andorra. Andorra is a little country between France and Spain where no one in our group had been before. Surely we could get into Spain through Andorra. There was no way we were going to make Madrid in time for the tournament. But we had other problems. No cash money to speak of between the five of us. We all had traveller's cheques and some leftover French francs but that was not going to help late at night in Andorra or in Spain. There was no place to change money until the banks opened the next day. And more of a concern, we had very little fuel in the hippie mobile. We were not going to be able to buy fuel late at night in the middle of nowhere even if we had some Spanish pesestas. Yes, you could say we had not planned this journey too well. And we were dead tired, hungry and heading in the wrong direction. Great.

We cruised into a tiny mountain village at about three in the morning. Cruised was the appropriate term because we were out of fuel. Running on empty just like the hit song around that time by Jackson Browne. No fuel. No money. Nothing open, anyway. "Kok" came to the rescue. The streetwise country boy knew what to do. After freewheeling into this sleeping village we double-parked next to a Citroën. "Kok" disappeared into somebody's back yard and returned with a garden hose he had cut up with his ever-present Swiss Army knife. Like a pro who had done this a hundred times he quickly siphoned off a tank of fuel from the parked Citroen. We were ecstatic and nervous now, eager to find that mysterious checkpoint wherever it was. "Kok" should have been a mercenary or a guerrilla rather than a tennis pro. Later on, he actually did join the Australian regular army after his tennis playing days were over. His true calling perhaps.

Eventually after following those tiny red lines on our map we came to a checkpoint early in the morning. It was an alpine douane but was it a French checkpoint, Spanish or Andorran? Whatever it was, it was very closed. The barriers were up; there was no human movement, only a couple of German Shepherd dogs prowling around. We could not guess when it would open up in the morning or into which country we were headed. And we were on court that morning sometime in Madrid, which was still many miles away. At least we still had fuel but now we were very tired and hungry. Also it was snowing up there, bitterly cold in the mountains. Yet again, I had another brilliant idea. Why not just drive through. Screw the immigration officials. They probably had guns again anyway like in Irún and would not let us in when they opened up. Who would let us in if they saw this band of hippies approaching?

The dogs were prowling around but I tested the barriers. They were mechanical ones so I simply lifted them up. Too easy. Wayne put the van in neutral and with a little push we silently cruised into some unknown country. Madrid here we come. No alarms went off, the dogs didn't savage us, so off we went.

Everyone was elated. Welcome to Espana. Don't forget to turn your clocks back 25 years. Another 600-700 kilometres and we would be there.

Our joy was short-lived. A couple of kilometres down the road we suddenly noticed two motorcyclists on our tails. They were ominously dressed like Spanish border police. Uh-oh. We were in deep doo-doo. These guys looked mean with dark uniforms, dark glasses, and handguns. Definitely SS, Gestapo or something more sinister perhaps. The bikers pulled us over. They did not even speak or wanted to speak any language to us. No English here, these dudes looked mean. How about a bribe? Well, they say it works in Mexico why not in Spain, same language, right. Oh, I forget, we did not have any pesetas and they surely would not accept a bribe in £ sterling traveller's cheques. They gestured for us to get out of the van and put all of our belongings on the side of the road in a pile. It was quite a sight. There were 75 racquets, a tennis-stringing machine, over 1000 sets of natural gut strings (Wayne the ever gung-ho salesman was hawking these expensive strings all over Europe) and piles of tennis gear. Spain in those days really came down hard on any drug influence into their little idealistic police State. We must have appeared to be hippies to these gendarmes. Of course they failed to find any drugs on us. The tennis strings were a bit of a mystery to them as it would be to most people. They even squeezed out the toothpaste tubes from our luggage looking for something that resembled hallucinogens. No luck. It was like two blind men at night searching a dark room for a black cat that wasn't really there. The only thing that had their full attention was a couple of Playboy magazines (banned in Spain, of course). I swear they weren't really mine. After an hour or so of fruitless searching our boys in black confiscated our Playboys and sped off back in the direction of that mysterious border which we had recently crossed. What luck, no bribes to pay and no penalty for sneaking in the back door uninvited.

I found out the following year the Customs limit for tennis racquets into Spain was a strict maximum of three per person. It did not matter if they were your tools of trade. Anything over that the number was liable for import duty. That means we were 60 racquets in excess that day. Remember, it always helps to keep a few playboy magazines handy to appease the customs officials. I suspect our gendarme friends were not tennis players because they did not know about rackets or catgut.

On the road again. We did make it to Madrid, eventually. It was much farther than we figured from Monte Carlo on the French

Riviera to Madrid in central Spain. We were close to Madrid the next day without further mishap, just a flat tyre. We spent the night in a small hotel on the outskirts of the city. Wayne had called the tournament director at the Campo de Tennis and explained that the Aussie contingent was running a tad late. The good news: he said it was OK to be a day late; the bad news: the only guy in the tournament was Gardiner. The other guys had missed the qualifying rounds, unfortunately. I was scheduled to play early next morning. We cruised into town the next day, found the Club de Campo somehow, and I literally went straight from the Hippie Mobile onto court. Nice preparation. My opponent was the rising young Spanish star, Jose Higueras, the wunderkind who was the next clay court champion out of Spain. I lost in three sets and gave it a pretty good effort. My preparation was not ideal, no warm-up, not much sleep or food in the past 36 hours, but nevertheless, Jose was too tough on clay. He had a wonderful backcourt game and would one day become the seventh ranked player in the world and a French Open finalist.

A bit depressing, the tournament was over for us almost as it started. It was tough too after the stressful journey to get to Madrid and very rough on the guys who were not even getting a start. Maybe the team should have hit the small tournaments somewhere in France rather than attack two of the biggest events in Europe during the spring, Monte Carlo and Madrid, back to back. Oh well, back to the drawing board.

Our next tournament was a smaller one, thank goodness, in a small town on the edge of Barcelona, called Sabadell. It was still a week away but at last everyone had hospitality and a little money guarantee in Sabadell.

As I said we were a little down. It's quite a downer when you are eliminated early in a tournament. A week to kill and no money coming in. It was even tougher on the rookies who were not getting to hit a ball even in anger. Poor "Blue". First time to Europe and the poor bugger had hardly hit a ball and gone through a lot of "Aggro".

A couple of days later we were having a quiet cerveza in a little sleazy bar adjacent to our pensione. Another Aussie, Bob Rheinberger ("Rhino") joined us for a beer. Bob was a true blue Aussie and a real country bloke; typically down to earth and genuine. "Rhino" later on gave me the oil on this kid McEnroe who had beaten him in the Paris qualifying.

Somehow we moved onto the subject of drinking. The dour-looking locals around us at the bar did not appear to be drinking up like you would see in an Australian pub. None of us were remotely like the typical Aussie whose few beers could be anything up to 15 or 20. In fact we were all lightweights. I was a very poor drinker (my parents never drank and I never inherited any urge to drink much).

Suddenly we are in a three-way contest to see who was the best drinker: Wayne, Rhino and myself. Crazy. The other three guys, Blue, Kok and Alan abstained. Why I was in there, I'll never know. Poor "Blue" had experienced a rough debut on the continent. He had not played many tennis matches yet, had a nightmare car trip and now he was experiencing a real bout of Spanish tummy.

"Blue" had not ever tasted a beer in his young career. Surprisingly the other guys, the supposed wild ones were sitting this one out. In our little three-way contest, the drink of choice was Bacardi rum. Probably rum, because it was dirt cheap—100 pesetas, the equivalent of $US1.30 for a large bottle—and we were very tight on money now. We had three of those bottles plus three small coke bottles. "Kok" was our referee and mixed the drinks, Bacardi and coke, proportionately. The rules were simple: last man standing was the champion (of what, I still do not know.)

After about 30 minutes there was no Bacardi left and the miniscule coke bottles had disappeared. We were very drunk. The other two guys were much bigger than I was and much stouter. I think, being lean almost skinny, I became drunk much quicker.

I still don't know who won the contest. But I know I was very ill and probably had acute alcohol poisoning. My doubles partner, Alan, heaved me up over his shoulders and carried me up three flights of stairs to my room. I dived on the flimsy bed which actually broke into two pieces. I lay in the "V" vomiting all night and could not move from that position for a long time. Never have I felt so miserable—I wanted to die in Spain and I almost did. The other two guys bounced back quite well even though they were very ill as well. I lay around for a few days feeling miserable, coughing up blood and stuff. It was very dumb and my health suffered for a few months after that. Never again. Never rum. Never again.

Time to move on. I was not too keen on the 450km journey from Madrid to Sabadell in the Hippie Mobile especially in my condition and cramped up in this small van. I was calling myself the winner of the drinking match but I was certainly paying the price of victory.

I don't recall too much of the Sabadall tournament. A nice little club with the very laid back atmosphere of a smaller event.

Until our fateful doubles match Alan and I had teamed up for the first time and we had tentative arrangements to play a lot together, including Wimbledon later on in June. Wayne and Kok were an established team. Poor "Blue" was on the outer once more with no partner.

As I said this was a genteel little tournament. We all had a little deal, probably the equivalent of around $US50 each and the all-important full hospitality. There was not much extra prize money to speak of. Probably a big trophy—they loved those big trophies in Spain—and maybe a few bottles of Bacardi rum thrown in too !

In our virginal doubles encounter Alan and I lost to my drinking adversary "Rhino" and another Aussie, Ernie Ewert ("Evert"). Ernie was a wonderful guy from Melbourne. The French and Spanish could not get their tongue around the name Ewert, the closest they could get was Evert, hence the nickname.

We lost fair and square to Rhino and Evert. No one witnessed our match on a backcourt at the Sabadell Club de Tennis. As it eventuated, these guys wanted to get out of town a little early. They had an invitation to another tournament, another guarantee, down in Malaga in the south of Spain. This tournament was starting in a day or so. The boys decided to award Alan and myself the win, picked up their small guarantee in Sabadell, and were on the cattle train out of there to Malaga.

Great, everyone was happy. We adjusted the result of our match and the other guys were gone. Our next match was to be a disaster. We were scheduled to play two Spanish players that Friday evening on Campo Centrale. One of the opponents, Rafael Ruiz, was completing his National Army service in Barcelona so he could not get there until the evening for his match. The other opponent was Juan Herrera, a bit of a gypsy, we presumed.

We were having a nice fun match. At 4-4 we broke the Spaniards and changed ends to serve out the set. However, on the crucial break point we had inadvertently called their shot long as it passed us at net. It was our call as there was no central umpire. It's hard to understand why the tournament officials did not have an umpire for a feature match and with quite a good crowd watching.

On the changeover Herrera went to check out our call and he discovered the ball had left a mark on the clay. It had ticked the baseline, barely. He summoned us back to check out the evidence. It was not an intentional bad call but it was the wrong call. Irrefutable evidence. What to do? Go back and replay the point or carry on? I said to Alan, why not go back and replay the thing. Who cares, there is very little prize money at stake, just some pride and ego involved. That would be an honourable thing to do. "No f..ing way" was Alan's reply. "It's our call, screw them"

The tension was palpable now as we prepared to serve out the set. It did not help when Herrera hit three balls to a far corner rather than give them to the server, Alan. Alan responded by knocking all three balls into a barranca out back of the court. War had been declared.

We did win the set but early in the second set things were not getting much better between Haswell and Herrera. Rafa Ruiz was a very nice guy who had been educated at an American college on a tennis scholarship.

He beckoned for Alan to come up to the net and have a chat. He was going to mediate things between his gypsy (no speak English) partner and the hot-headed Aussie. Rafa said "Hey guys, this is just a fun match, not that important who wins it, so why not stop acting like a bastard?"

Alan snapped. That boxer was coming out in him. Another B word from Rafa and then the two of them were facing off across the net. Alan dropped his racquet and smashed him in the mouth. Lots of blood and teeth everywhere. Rafa was obviously totally shocked and hurt. I was totally shocked too. He struggled to his feet somehow and said something bad this time in his native tongue. Crunch. Another sickening blow to the jaw. This time, Rafa stayed down, out cold poor guy. We later learned his jaw was broken.

I was right there next to the antagonists. Herrera was sulking somewhere down the back of his court. Alan had hit the wrong guy. Rafa was just trying to smooth things out between these two guys and he gets KO'd, poor bugger.

Pandemonium broke out. Dozens of Spanish spectators were running on the court calling for the policia. Alan was ready to fight all of them. He said "Come on Aggro, help me out here" I think he was serious. You are talking to a guy who never had one real scrap at school. Now you want me to take on about 100 Spanish dudes? And to top it off we are in the land of the Generalissimo where the foreigner was always in the wrong. It was even rumoured if you had a car accident in Spain in those times, they would lock you up and ask questions later (most tourists purchased a bail bond before travelling to Spain). Shit Alan, could you have picked a worse place to do this? On a tennis court where gentlemen play the game then traditionally shake hands after the match. And in bloody Spain to boot.

Alan had one bit of luck on his side. The tournament director was not a Spaniard, but a Colombian guy. We all knew Willie "Pato" Alvarez. He must have lived in that part of Spain when he wasn't playing tournaments around Europe. Willie was a legend but a real nutter. He had been doing this for 20 years, playing tournaments all over the Continent and selling everything he could from tennis racquets, to tennis gut, to jock straps. Willie was very eccentric and a gay blade (he had propositioned me later on somewhere in Spain). What a character when he played with a big beer belly held up with a black belt and he also would pull every possible gamesman trick on court. One of his favourites and the crowd's favourite was rattling his dentures when he was returning serve. Funny as hell, but tough to play against. Supposedly he had wins over all the best players in the world on clay court. He probably drove them so crazy they tanked to him.

Willie realised the gravity of the situation. He moved Alan off court quickly and saved him (and me) from a lynching by the mob. Poor Rafa. When the medical people finished with him, he had to report back to his barracks in Barcelona. Willie just told Alan to get out of town quickly otherwise he would be dead meat. Alan went back to the hotel and was on a train to Switzerland within the hour. His parting words were "Sorry, we did not finish the match mate. Could you pick up my appearance money ($50) for me?" "Good luck getting that, mate" I replied. See you at Wimbledon if you are out of jail.

The next day the big score board adjacent to the clubhouse had posted the doubles results: Gardiner-Haswell: disqualified, in bold red lettering. Pretty embarrassing. The irony of it all was we should not have been out there; it should have been Rheinberger-Ewert playing the match. Alan and I played two matches in our careers together. Our record: one loss, one DQ. We never played Wimbledon as a team; in fact we never played together again.

Thank goodness those two weeks were over. I escaped from Spain back to play some tournaments in England. Bad things seemed to happen in Spain.

As for Alan Haswell, his tennis career was virtually over before he really started. He played some inter-club tennis matches in Switzerland that spring after he had fled from Spain. A few months later, the International Tennis Federation (I.T.F.) gave him a one year ban from tournaments worldwide. Scratch Wimbledon for us (I did play singles though, in 1972). The Spanish Tennis Federation banned Alan for life. He could never compete in Spain again. Apparently Rafael Ruiz was a member of the Real Club de Tennis in Barcelona and was good friends with the president of the Spanish Federation from that Club. I never saw him again, poor bugger. I wonder if he ever played tennis again when he recovered from his injuries?

Tennis is and always has been a gentleman's game. I had never heard of anyone resorting to fisticuffs on the court. The worst I had ever seen was some name-calling and threats on court and then maybe refusing the mandatory hand shake at match end. But never the fists, or a racquet over the head.

In 1969 my first year overseas there was some action in the locker room in Berlin. Roger Taylor, the broad shouldered Englishman from a steel working family in Sheffield had a go at the Aussie Bob Hewitt. Hewitt was the Dr Jeckyl of the tennis courts. Another big man, he was psychotic on the court but a very soft-spoken gentleman off the court. In Berlin, Hewitt had berated Roger all match (Hewitt won the match) and then he continued the abuse in the locker room. Roger had a gutful and finally gave him a left hook.

Hewitt had a cut to his face but Roger broke his hand. He missed the French Open the next week. Maybe he felt some satisfaction though.

I'm surprised no one, player or official, had not smacked down Nastase or McEnroe over the years. One year at Wimbledon, I was watching the centre court match with McEnroe versus Brad Gilbert on TV. It was getting very intense and ugly (by the way, Gilbert is the author of the tennis book *Winning Ugly*). Bud Collins, the famous American tennis historian and reporter for the Boston Globe, was doing some colour commentary for the US TV channel covering Wimbledon. One of the other commentators asked Bud if anyone had ever completely lost it on court and smacked someone. It appeared it might happen this day on centre court Wimbledon. Bud replied he had never seen such an incident, but he heard about these two young Australians who were involved in actual fisticuffs on court, down in Spain, back in 1972. One of the Aussies, Alan Haswell, was a good amateur boxer and KO'd one of the opposing Spaniards. Tactfully Bud said the name of the other Australian escaped him (thanks Bud for saving my name—he knew who the other player was, I think). In his book, Bud documented our match in Sabadell but never mentioned me by name. But the commentators agreed it was the single worst incident in International tennis to date. What a great legacy to own.

I did give Spain another chance a couple of years later. However, I had another harrowing experience in Madrid. A crazy guy in a bar attacked Ernie Evert and myself. He slapped us around a bit and then chased us out wielding a knife. We never did find out his motivation, perhaps because we were foreigners, but we left the scene quickly. No more Spain for me. It was much easier exiting Spain than entering Spain.

A footnote to the Alan Haswell story: I ran into him a few years later at the New South Wales Hardcourt championships in a place called Orange, NSW. Apparently he had gone back into the ring in

Sydney to do some more boxing seeing his tennis days were over. In one particular bout he had his eye messed up quite badly and was now wearing glasses. He said boxing was a fool's game and he had retired from it, totally. Way to go Alan.

Alan was now traveling around the country centres of NSW representing one of the tennis racquet companies. He seemed very happy and was in Orange with his fiancée. We never discussed Spain, for some reason. The subject never came up.

Sometime later that year Alan was killed in a car accident coming back from a country town. What a tragic ending. He was only 20 something. His last tennis match overseas was cut short after one set, and his young life was cut short as it seemed, in the first set.

Chapter 7
Asian Journey

Tokyo

Travelling around South East Asia was a little different than travel in Europe and America. I really enjoyed it because the cities were so exotic. In the Orient the world was not the like the Western world. The only thing that seemed to connect with the West was the occasional McDonald's restaurant in the big cities. This was a whole new continent, so different than playing in Europe and in the States. Undoubtedly America was the best place to play tennis, so easy to travel between tournaments, the people are extremely friendly (and they can speak English. Well, American English at least) and things are so uniform. However, not such a big deal because there is a blandness after a while. Chicago is like Cleveland and Cleveland is like Atlanta. A lot of the same.

The Asian Circuit did not really get going until the mid 1970s. Admittedly, these were little tournaments here and there at random times of the year but now the Grand Prix Circuit had given some cohesion to these cities for an actual circuit in the last quarter of the year.

The circuit started in Maui, Hawaii (everyone's favourite) then wound down under to Australia for the Australian Indoors (in Sydney) then Melbourne, and Perth (Indoors) followed. The true Asian swing of the Circuit now started in Tokyo in October, then down through South East Asia to Hong Kong, Taipei, Manila,

Bangkok and finally to India for the last tournament. The Indian Open was rotated between the Indian cities of Bombay, Bangalore, New Delhi and Calcutta.

The first stop, Tokyo, was such an eye opener. I had never seen a city so big, so crowded and so foreign. Seemed like no one spoke English. At least in European cities, you could use a little French, German, or Spanish to get by and a lot of people spoke English, especially in the northern European countries. But in Japan things were alien to me. Even the street signs were in Japanese characters, naturally enough, so getting around was not easy. So much humanity wherever you turned But with all these teeming millions, the city seemed to work. This was not chaos like I was to later see in India, but total organisation. The Japanese system seemed to work, everyone was on a team, polite and looking out for each other. No one seemed to buck the system. Crime was negligible, apparently. Graft and corruption did not exist like in the other countries. One of the biggest cities on earth in population, yet it was safe and there were no concerns about getting mugged in Tokyo.

We could not believe, however, how expensive things were in Japan. Paris had nothing on this place. A small orange juice was setting us back the equivalent of $5 (and this was still the 1970s). I guess fresh fruit was at a premium in Japan. An apple or orange could cost us up to $10 each and in the Ginza district, you could buy a decorated gift box of fruit, say two cantaloupe for example, for something like $70 in our money!

Another thing that was a little astounding was the minute sized hotel rooms and beds. Some rooms were six feet across and the beds were obviously designed for midgets. The beds were never long enough. I'm no giant but I had trouble in those miniature beds. Poor Victor Amaya, the 6'7" American had such a tough time, having to move out of the official player hotel in Tokyo and find something bigger. He must have felt like Gulliver arriving in Lilliput.

The Japanese tennis racquet company, Yoneyama, was starting to make some moves in the international market around this time. They had been successful in the badminton and soft tennis market in Asia and now they were moving into the Australian and US markets. Mr Yoneyama decided to anglicise the name a tad and changed the brand name to Yonex. Yonex signed up quite a few of the Aussie players, including our big star, Tony Roche, and later on Martina Navratilova, the European superstar was contracted.

I was one of the lower ranked pros to get a deal with Yonex. My ATP ranking was fairly healthy at this time—somewhere in the world top 100—so I had a little contract. It was not huge money but it was not bad and they paid bonuses for doing well in bigger events and also if my ranking improved significantly throughout the year. It felt like Christmas coming to Tokyo and getting all the new model racquets and the latest clothing lines.

I did have some quite good results in the Japan open. The clay courts at Den en Chofu stadium were a bit like our Aussie ant bed so I did feel somewhat at home. However, apart from the court surface, conditions were somewhat tough. The weather was cold this time of year and the Japanese tennis balls flew a bit strangely. Maybe they were smaller than normal, too. And we were coming here after a couple of weeks indoors in Australia. No excuse, that's tennis, but that was one thing I always found difficult, adjusting to different conditions from week to week.

In the late 1970s, prior to the Japan Open, I lucked out on an invitation to play a special tournament down south in Fukuoka. I'm not too sure how this invite eventuated but I was approached by one of the Aussie players, Owen Davidson, who had a Japanese connection of sorts. "Davo" was one of Australia's star players of the 1960s, particularly in men's doubles and mixed doubles. He won the Grand Slam of mixed with Margaret (nee Smith) Court.

In these times "Davo" was the resident pro down in Texas at the Woodlands Tennis Club out of Houston. One of his tennis students, the son of a wealthy Japanese businessman, was doing his schooling and tennis training in Texas. This rich man owned the fabulous Kasuga Lawn Tennis Club in Fukuoka and he wished to invite Owen and one more Australian to his big tournament there in October. When I played at The Woodlands, after the US Open, in the doubles only event there, "Davo" asked me if I would like to go to Fukuoka before playing in Tokyo. Naturally, I said OK.

We were treated like superstars this week. We were met at Narita airport Tokyo, and flown by private jet to Fukuoka. It seemed like this Japanese man owned half the city. We were showered with gifts and were even invited to play golf at the local country club. We did appreciate that the average person in Japan will never get on a real golf course in their lifetime. This was quite an honour to be invited for a game of golf in Japan.

The Kasuga Tennis Club was designed on the four Grand Slams. There was a clay court surface just like at Roland Garros, a grass court like Wimbledon and Kooyong, and a hard court identical to those courts at Flushing Meadow, New York. As well, there were indoor clay courts. This club was very impressive to say the least.

In the tournament, the All Japan Professional Championship, "Davo" and I met in the quarter -finals. I managed to win—Davo did not play competitively much any more—but I think he was surprised I was not a total leper. I gathered this invitation was a nice gesture by our host, but not designed to upset the Japanese players in their final event of their seasonal circuit. After all, it was called the All Japan Championships.

When I won the semi-final, I was up against the number one player of Japan, Jun Kamiwazumi in the final. This was not good for the organisers, they wanted to see Kamiwazumi against the other Jun, Jun Kuki, the number two Japanese player. Not a gaijin, a foreigner, versus their golden boy. Perhaps this was the moment for "Davo" to whisper in my ear and ask me to roll over in the final. Guess he did not expect me to do much against Kamiwazumi.

Jun was an international star, having beaten the world number one player, Stan Smith (twice), a couple of years earlier.

The final was televised Nationally. Played indoors on the dirt courts. When I won in straight sets everyone was a little stunned and Jun was very pissed off. How could he possibly be losing to a Gaijin in their "closed" Masters finale? I was fine with the result. First prize was a lot of yen, about $US10,000 which was a lot of money for me in the 1970s. Plus the biggest trophy I have ever seen, apart from the Davis Cup, of course.

Thanks for the invite "Davo". I never did ask him if there was a big loss of face with the tournament host. I believe he wanted "Davo" to bring along a player of a level who would not upset the local stars, lose gracefully along the way, and subsequently not allow the locals to lose face. Strangely enough, they never did invite any foreigners back to Fukuoka after that debacle. Naturally,I was never invited back to defend my title.

Manila

Next stop, Manila, The Philippines. Manila was more of a typical Asian city. Extraordinary traffic, diesel fumes (from all the Jeepneys, the local taxis), chaos and confusion and terrible heat and humidity. I have never played tennis in a hotter place. Australia can get very hot in places. Once, I played at Kooyong in Melbourne during the Aussie Champs and the temperature reached 112°F (45°C) on the grass with strong dusty winds blowing. And in the States during July and August some of the cities on the summer circuit were brutally hot as well. The stops at Cincinnati, Louisville, Atlanta and Washington (D.C.) (where they had oxygen on the courts during change of ends) were particularly hot and humid. But Manila was the winner for sure. The qualifying matches for the Manila tournament at Rizal Memorial Stadium were played on clay/shell courts (who plays on shell anymore?). There was no shade, dazzling white courts in the hot sun, no place to hide. We sweated like water buffaloes. We were told not to drink the local water but the only other option was to drink carbonated drinks, probably not the best choice in that humidity. Between matches we would go back to the hotel rooms with the luxury of ceiling fans and flop into a lovely cold bath.

Fortunately no one died during "Qualies". Now I knew how those prisoners must have felt on the Bataan death march near Manila during the war. I was one of the two lucky guys to qualify. Then the tournament proper went indoors to a makeshift court inside Rizal Stadium, a basketball arena. Essentially, it was a tin shed with a few ceiling fans pushing the air around. The court was still shell and the lighting was very average. I think I preferred the white outside shell courts even though it was under the boiling sun. At least there was more air to suck in.

In my first time in Manila the draw was small but a very impressive field. Big names like Newcombe, Orantes, Solomon (USA) and Barrazutti (Italy), all good on clay. But could they play on shell? Why were they subjecting themselves to this torture? Maybe they though Manila might be a good place for a laid back holiday towards year's end. Or had they heard about those massage parlours?

My opening match in the tin shed was against Dick Dell, brother of the US Davis Cup captain Donald Dell, who was one of the big time tennis agents of the time. It was a good draw for the both of us considering the field. There must have been 3,000 spectators jammed in there, not much oxygen and not much light. In the middle of the match a hailstorm battered the tin shed. Now we could not hear a line call or anything whatsoever from the umpire. We could not see, hear or breathe very well. A fun match. Luckily I prevailed in three tie-breakers and did not suffer a heart attack. My next match was against the highly rated Corrado Barrazutti from Italy, one of the world's best clay courters. Looking at the scrawny little Italian, you would not think he could break an egg, but he was very good. For some inexplicable reason, but typical of Filipino organisation, we went back outside to play the match, the only match in the main draw played on the outside shell. Go figure. Barrazutti was a whiner at the best of times, always gesturing in the typical Italian manner, ever bitter with the world. Under these conditions, this was my chance for a win against a world top tenner. It must have been hilarious to see this match. We had one umpire, no linesmen, and one teenage ball boy with only one leg! Corrado was continually bitching at the sun, the court surface, the line calls and the slow moving ball boy, poor wretch. He beat me in the end. Later on, somewhere in Europe, Corrado's lovely wife told me she took some video of the match. She said it was hilarious, an amazingly funny match in those conditions. No spectators to speak of, just a few street urchins watching, a couple of dogs and Mrs Barrazutti. And, the poor ball boy struggling to do his best.

That was all I remember of that first Manila tournament. The main thing I took out this place of was the mind numbing humidity. Also, my former doubles partner, Ross Case, from "The Capital of the Tennis World, Toowoomba", won the tournament. Ross gutsed out the difficult conditions and beat John Newcombe in the final. What an extraordinary win. I think his smaller stature and great fitness helped in those trying conditions. He won again a year or so later in Manila. Definitely, he was king of the shell. Again the ant bed court experience growing up in Queensland helped, I'm sure.

Another memory of the Philippines was our visit to the faith healer. We had all heard about those miraculous cures. Yes, there were some fraudulent healers. But this one particular man, a Mr Juan Blanche, had done amazing stuff with two of our Aussie tennis greats, Tony Roche and Phil Dent. "Rochie" had tried the knife on his ailing elbow but nothing could rid the dreaded tennis elbow. After flying to Manilla, Tony visited Mr Blanche and was born again. His elbow was cured and his great career had a new lease of life. Was it faith? There was no payment required for the surgery. Was it psychosomatic? Who was this Catholic mystery man and why was he healing anyway?

We had to find out. One morning around 4am a bunch of tennis players, Australians and Americans mainly, piled into some taxis and headed for the slums on the edge of Manila. Some of us had chronic injuries like most players carry and some of us were just curious onlookers. We eventually found the little Catholic Church. The church was already filled with locals and a few foreigners in the pre-dawn darkness. That is when the faith healer supposedly had his healing powers.

I was hanging out in the pews of the church with another Aussie, John Bartlett (J.B.) and Russell Simpson ("sheepdog") a kiwi friend and my doubles partner at the time. We were pretty much in the curious onlooker category. Eventually someone beckoned for us to come back into a little room in the back of the church to see the "Man". Suddenly it became a little embarrassing because we were three patients without legitimate health issues. What to do? Maybe he could fix my ailing backhand. However, I did have a chronic lower back problem so I spoke up first, while Russell looked sheepish and J.B. stood silent. Mr Blanche said he already knew about my back injury before I walked into the room. OK, righto. He then proceeded to put his thumb on the exact spot on one side of my back and gave me a tremendous crack without any effort. He said "Go son, you will be fine". J.B. then found some courage to enquire about a benign cyst on his neck (he already knew it was benign from his father who was a doctor in Australia). Blanche took a quick look and said to J.B. come back tomorrow and he would operate. Blanche intimated my finger would be the scalpel. J.B. did not return the next day. He did not relish the idea of another two-hour taxi ride each way plus the thought of me operating on his neck!

It was an eerie experience. And there were the newspaper cuttings on the wall, Blanche with Newcombe and Roche. We heard wonderful stories of people getting out of wheelchairs and walking for the first time. People recovering from leukaemia and some getting their sight restored. It worked for Tony Roche. As for me, my back was great for the remainder of the Asian tour. You gotta have faith, I guess.

That was the Philippines. I did not know it then but I was to return in later years, just like General MacArthur, and spend quite a bit of time in the Islands in a coaching capacity.

Hong Kong

This was definitely one of the fun weeks for the players on the Asian Tour and particularly so for the wives and girlfriends. Weeks out from the Hong Kong tournament, everyone was discussing what they were going to buy there. Usually it was jewellery, Rolex watches (the real gold ones), suits made to order and all kinds of stereos, Walkmans, etc. My favourite buy was the suits. It involved a ferry ride across the island to mainland Kowloon where you ordered your specifications from some hole in the wall shop in the alleyways. 24 hours later, the suits would be delivered to your hotel and at extraordinary reasonable prices.

Everyone saved money in Hong Kong. You spent a fortune but think of all the money you were saving if you bought the same stuff back home. Not a great rationale but it kept the players' partners content.

The tennis matches were played in Victoria Park right amidst the skyscrapers, hotels and other tall buildings. There was always a mass of people everywhere you went. I have no memorable matches from Hong Kong—I conveniently forget my losses, once again—but one match stands out mainly because it was a debacle of sorts.

My match was a centre court match against Gene Mayer from the USA. Gene was an unorthodox player, double fisted both sides, and very difficult to play against because of the unorthodoxy. He was one of the first guys to use the ridiculously large headed (or so it seemed) Prince tennis racquet and he used it very well indeed, streaking to number four in the world in quick time. Gene was a nice enough guy but he strutted around the court like he had a Prince racquet lodged somewhere up his butt.

The tournament organisers this particular year were training the local Chinese to officiate the matches and training the local kids to be ball boys and ball girls, a first. Normally the expatriates from the UK or the USA were the court officials, but not this time. Gene and myself were to be the guinea pigs, the opening match on centre court. There were horrendous line calls from the start. Everyone was up tight. And why did virtually every Chinese person, young or old, wear glasses? Even the ball kids were tense. The match was deteriorating and the central umpire had effectively lost control of his staff. I was getting a bit frustrated (Aggroed?) and Gene was becoming more obnoxious than usual. As I prepared to serve in a critical point of the first set, I turned to the ball girl for the balls. She just held one ball in her hand, frozen like a statue, just staring out behind her glasses at me, poor thing. No movement whatsoever, no ball for me. I think she had the yips in her first time out there. The crowd were yelling stuff to her and to make light of the situation. I, literally, quietly tiptoed over to her and prised the ball gently out from her hand. To the delight of the spectators.

But then she just fainted. It was very hot out there too. Down for the count, poor girl. The whole thing must have been too much for her. I felt like an ass and the match went downhill after that for me. We were both insensitive bastards because we never did check on the girl's welfare after the match. At least one of us could have bought her a milkshake or flowers or something.

Still on Gene Mayer. Now this guy could eat. Gene and his brother, Sandy, also a World top ten player could pack it away. It was the stuff of legend. One day during the Hong Kong event, a group of us went on an organised boat adventure around the island to Stanley Markets and some other spots on the island. Well, to our luck, we espied the golden arches of McDonalds on the shores. Someone in our group made the excursion to the shore to get us some lunch. Gene and his wife were in the boat and while most people were putting in the typical order of say one hamburger, medium fries and a milkshake, Gene ordered twelve Big Macs, a few milkshakes and all kinds of extra fries. No worries, he scoffed the lot and that was just a mere snack for him this afternoon on the boat.

Gene was not a big fat guy by any means but a top professional athlete and obviously in shape. He must have had quite a metabolism and quite a food bill each week. Another story of the Mayer brothers was during Wimbledon one year. Staying at the very fashionable Dorchester Hotel in Park Lane, London they absolutely scoffed a whole leg of lamb at the buffet dinner. The restaurant manager asked them to leave after they went back and back until nothing was left. Sometimes Sandy would order all the main courses on a restaurant menu, maybe five or six dishes at once.

Talking of eating, another outing during the Hong Kong week was a trip to the mansion of Henry Fok for a traditional Chinese banquet. Henry was an amazingly wealthy local figure, rumoured to have made his fortune though the opium trade as well as from his gambling casinos. One of the main characters in James Clavell's epic novel *Nobel House.* set in Hong Kong, is based on Henry Fok's life. He was a lover of tennis and patron of the Hong Kong Lawn Tennis Association. Maybe a frustrated tennis player because even though he could not win his club tournament, he nevertheless had a huge trophy made and presented to himself. It was a replica of the Wimbledon trophy with a solid gold Slazenger tennis ball on top. Might be worth a bit at today's gold prices. Not that Henry was ostentatious by any stretch, but he did have a ton of the best Burmese jade in the foyer of his monstrous mansion.

The traditional Chinese banquet was very lavish, very scrumptious. There were over twelve courses. No menu. Just course after course would come out served by Mr Fok's numerous staff members. We recognised some dishes, like shark fin soup and duck, but most dishes were a mystery, which we dutifully ate. One of the American players Tom Gullikson fished out a bird's head from his soup. Apparently that is a lucky omen to score the bird's head. He was happily tossing it back and forth amongst the other players in the room. I cannot recall how Tom did that week in the tournament or if he had some good karma in Hong Kong.

Everyone was a little squeamish at the end of the banquet when we were informed of the dishes. There was dog, exotic bear's paw and other disgusting stuff like offal. I think my Chinese food eating days were over right then. Even when I lived in Singapore years later I never opted for Chinese fare very often (only if I knew what it was).

Canton

Around this time in the late 1970s the People's Republic of China was just discovering this game called tennis. They knew about table tennis but now they were interested in the bigger version and not the one played on a table. The inaugural Chinese Open, an A.T.P. sanctioned event, was played in Canton (known as Guangzhou) and I recall this was about 1980. The same week as this tournament, Bjorn Borg and our Aussie, John Alexander (J.A.) were playing a series of exhibitions in China. Tennis was coming to this land.

Canton is not far from Hong Kong, roughly 55 miles as the crow flies. You'd think this would be a pretty easy journey even in 1980. Well, this was one of the most arduous journeys I have ever taken. It outdid some of the cattle train journeys I took across the top of Spain or down the boot of Italy. Just through sheer time and aggravation. Amazingly, it took twelve hours.

Coincidentally there was a big trade show in Canton the same week as the tournament. There were absolutely no seats available on any plane coming into Canton. One exception was Jimmy Connors (and his sidekick/buddy Lornie Kuhle). Jimmy and Lornie were granted plane travel. Connors was probably getting a province in China or more for playing in this tournament and there was no way he was doing the twelve hour trek especially if he knew about this horror. Jimmy wanted a commercial flight or private jet or he was not playing China.

All the other players had to do the tough travel. Some were coming in from the States, Europe or South America . Unknowingly they had this little bonus trip after getting into Hong Kong. The first leg of the journey was by hydrofoil to Macau, the former Portuguese island colony. I guess that was the closest place where the People's Republic of China had an Embassy and we had to have that entry visa to get in. Our little group of players had a few European guys among us and there were some passport issues with a couple of them. So after two or three hours of stuffing around we finally had our rubber stamps and were on our way. There were some question whether we would get into China because the border closed down around 5pm. We barely squeaked through in time (I had visions of Andorra and Spain eight years earlier).

The second leg was by bus. This was horrendously slow at night. For some reason the bus only travelled at about 30 miles an hour with insufficient headlights. The roads were crowded with people and water buffalo pulling carts, also numerous animals, you name it, they crowded that narrow road. In addition, we had to cross the meandering Pearl River three times before reaching Canton. There were no bridges spanning the Pearl, a very wide river, but there were ferries of sorts. And we had to wait each time for the ferry to return and make our slow crossing. Three separate crossings for goodness sake.

We did stop for dinner somewhere. Seemed like there were Chinese restaurants everywhere. I did not partake of the food because when we entered the restaurant there were rats running out the front door. If the rats were running away, it must have been really bad food.

We did finally make it too Canton twelve hours after leaving Hong Kong. I thought our little group must have been unlucky. However on talking to other players who came in on subsequent excursions, taking the same route, their journeys were approximately the same length. The horror!

I'm sure China has developed in leaps and bounds (the great leap forward?) in the past 30 years or so. I've heard the hotels and restaurants in the bigger cities like Beijing and Shanghai are absolutely first class nowadays. They have undoubtedly have McDonalds restaurants as well.

Our little hotel in Canton that year was very spartan. I'm sure all those businessmen who were there for the trade convention snagged the best rooms in the best hotels. Another mistake we made was to request Western food like bacon and eggs for breakfast. We should have just stuck to fish and rice. I wonder where Connors and Lorne stayed? Never did find out.

My roommate and travel companion on this trip was another Aussie, Cliff Letcher from Melbourne. Cliff or "Flash" as he was known was a big lumbering guy with blonde hair, strong as a bull with quite an impish nature. He was very popular on the tour. "Flash" played the tough guy but really he was a gentle giant. He received his moniker due to his penchant for flashing, mooning or showing off his bum. Any place, any time. His best moon job was yet to come later on the courts of Bangalore during the Indian Open, the last leg of the Asian tour. He had embarrassed me no end during the tournament in Manila earlier. Four of the Aussies including "Flash" and myself were having dinner in a lavish restaurant at the Philippine plaza hotel on Manila Bay. We were guests of Mrs Imelda Marcos at one of her Marcos-owned hotels. During dinner we were serenaded at our table by a trio of Filipino singers who were wandering from table to table. "Flash" thought these guys were intimating we were two gay couples out to dinner. He was a little pissed and dropped his pants as well. Gave them a full moon right there at the table. I've never felt so small and never have I seen so many astounded diners. Our serenaders never missed a beat (went straight into playing "Moon over Manila" or some appropriate tune.)

I actually did not play singles in Canton. Just doubles that week. The qualifying tournament was held in Hong Kong to facilitate things (and save the poor non-qualifiers the ordeal of the twelve hour trek into China). I was held up in Brisbane during the previous week playing doubles and had missed the qualifying deadline. It was probably a good thing because I had just undergone eye surgery a week or two earlier (for a pterygium, common to tennis players, farmers and other people exposed to our harsh Australian outdoors) and was not up to playing much tennis just yet.

To complicate my condition, I arrived in Hong Kong late at night from Brisbane, threw my prescribed drops in my eye before crashing in the hotel. Unfortunately I had used the wrong drops from a similar small bottle which was for my athlete's foot condition, chronic tinea. My poor eye took a while to recover from that mishap.

I did get to play doubles though. Connors won the tournament, naturally. He usually did. Obviously Jimmy was probably more rested and better fed than everyone else. The best news was everyone had a chance to fly out of Canton. The bad news was it was

CACC airlines, old crates but we made it safely. No more busses for us. Our plane was going to the other China, the Republic of China, Taiwan.

Taipei

It was a little confusing. Taiwan and Hong Kong were both Chinese countries but not recognised by Mainland China as one of their own. Coming into Taipei from Guangzhou, the immigration officials were not impressed some players retained their loose leafed Chinese visa in their passports, rather than toss them away. This was similar to a situation in the past when I went out of Israel to one of the neighbouring Arab countries like Lebanon or Egypt. The Arabs did not want to see the loose leafed Israeli visa. Peculiarly, the Israelis did not care if you were entering their country after being in a neighbouring Arab country.

No worries, we all made it into Taiwan. How many names can this place go by? There was Republic of China (ROC), Taiwan (formerly Formosa) and Chinese Taipei. The weather was invariably bad in Taipei at this time of year so the matches were held indoors. Tennis seemed boring inside, not much excitement for the fans or the players. Shopping in Taipei held more excitement. One of the highlights of that week was going off the beaten tourist path and visiting the Chinese medicinal shops at a street called Snake Alley. Snake Alley had all the traditional cures that probably had been passed down for 5000 years or more in Chinese medicine. One of their little potions to ward off cancer was a snake's blood concoction. The unfortunate snakes, hanging alive on hooks from the shop ceiling, were slit open then some blood was extracted and poured into a little glass. Then more liquid was added from a decanter, which appeared to have a lizard floating in it. The old men would come into the shop, ordered a shot and then, cheers, bottoms up. Possibly good for a hangover as well. I could have really used a shot of that down in Madrid in 1972.

Another medicinal cure we saw, to cure asthma apparently, was the swallowing of a rat foetus, dipped in honey. Simply slide it down the throat: no more asthma. Just the thought of a baby rat going down would kill any hint of asthma, I suspect.

Bangkok

Bangkok. We were getting close now to the end of the Asian Circuit and getting close to the end of the tennis year. One more stop after Thailand then off to India and it was homeward bound for much needed rest before the Australian summer circuit.

If we thought Manila had terrible traffic congestion and severe pollution from those diesel fumes then Bangkok may have surpassed it. And the heat and humidity was on par with Manila. Luckily the tennis matches were held indoors (with air conditioning) which made things a tad more humane. The only problem was getting from the hotel to the indoor stadium. The journey could take 45 minutes or it could take three hours. If there was a downpour the streets would become flooded in no time and nobody would move for ages. Apparently the city is so low and the drainage is very poor. It's the Venice of the East.

One doubles match I played in Bangkok was a bit crazy and a little embarrassing. My partner this particular week (why did it seem I had a different doubles partner every week?) was the silky smooth Indian, my friend Sashi Menon. Sashi was a fine player, one of the best to come out of India in this era, and he had learned his trade playing college tennis at USC in Los Angeles, California.

We had teamed up before. This time our opening match was against the local wildcards PanomKorn and Sombat. These guys were OK but not Grand Prix standard so this should have been a routine win for Sashi and me. However, we were both in poor form, lacking in confidence and somehow not communicating on the court. We could not scratch ourselves against the local yokels "Wombat" and "Popcorn" (their first names were simply unpronounceable to Westerners, hence those nicknames).

We looked so laughable out there. The crowd thought we were tanking to the home team. Little did they know we were trying our butts off. After a while, the crowd was booing and jeering at us, our tank job looked so obvious. We blew a dozen chances to close out the match then lost in three tight sets. Sashi was chuckling to himself at how farcical this match had become. He was saying "Come on Aggro, let's just end this misery" but I was dying inside. Seriously, I was trying but it was not there. It was embarrassing and the crowd gave us heaps. The humiliation did not end there; the press even roasted us next day for our blatant tank to the local boys. You would think they would praise their local boys for such a nice result. Sorry, Sashi. I think our partnership ended on that ignominious defeat in Bangkok.

Bangalore

We dragged ourselves off to India for a final tournament. Most of the players were a bit punch drunk by this time and were so ready for home and rest. However, the Indian Lawn Tennis body had thrown in a nice lure to entice players to play the Indian Open. Their sponsor, the national airline, Air India, was donating an around-the-world air ticket on Air India for any participant in the tournament. This was quite attractive for most of us who were not earning a lot of dollars.

My first trip to India in 1976 was to Bangalore, Southern India. Each year they rotated the tournament between the big cities of Bombay, New Delhi, Calcutta as well as Bangalore.

Because of the British influence tennis was quite popular on the subcontinent and cricket was even bigger. India had produced some great players over the years and they were very useful on grass courts. The surface of choice in Bangalore was not grass, but cow dung. Yes, that is correct, cow dung. However, it was not as crappy a surface as it seemed. I think it was a better surface than the shell courts of the Philippines. Just remember to come prepared with a tetanus shot in case you fell over and scraped yourself. All part of being a touring professional, the ability to be able to adapt to different court surfaces and different conditions. More of a concern to me was the locally made tennis balls. I swear Matchless tennis balls were not round; they seem to wobble in flight. It was such a great name Matchless because the balls were indeed without a match.

The stadium in Bangalore was not huge, just a couple of cow dung courts adjacent to each other and seating for about 5000 people. But every day of the tournament it was packed, a sea of dark faces. The Indians came out in droves just like they do at cricket matches. Well, you would expect a few to show up in the world's second most populous country.

The Indian stars of this era were the Amritraj brothers from nearby Madras (but now out of Hollywood), my ex doubles partner, Sashi Menon and Ramesh Krishnan. Ramesh's Dad, Ramanathan Krishnan was a world-class player during the previous decade.

As it turned out I had to play Anand Amritraj the eldest of the brothers. Vijay was the middle brother and a top ten player in the world. Ashok, the younger brother was a fine player too.

Playing against Anand on home soil (or home cow dung, rather) was quite an experience. It could have been a scene from a Bollywood movie. Apparently the locals perceived Anand as a flamboyant playboy, somebody from humble roots and caste who had turned his back on their society for the high life.

Now he was a tennis star more at home in Hollywood, Los Angeles than in his home country. Anand was decked out usually in a lovely lavender or a canary yellow tennis outfit and bedecked in gold chains. He even looked the part of a Bollywood or Hollywood movie mogul {his later calling after the tennis touring days). Though Vijay was always Mr Cool on court, Anand seemed to be forever prissy and often with a scowl on his face. The crowd ripped into the "Purple Peacock" the name they had dubbed him.

At the same moment on the adjacent dunger, my good buddy "Flash" was playing one of the Americans. "Flash" hated cow dung. He was not the best mover on any surface and now he was like a bull on roller skates. He kept falling down. When he went down "Flash" would pull his shorts and jocks down below his knees. Luckily he had a tetanus shot. I'm not sure who or what his moon was intended for, the court or the crowd, but the big crowd was simply loving it. Cries of "Show us your arse Letcher" would go up around the stadium every time he went down. This was not a pretty sight. It was very difficult to concentrate next to this scene as well as the roars from the crowd. Anand was bitching at everything and everyone, including the noise, and the crowd attacked him. He was the villain; "Flash" became a hero that day.

I ended up winning but poor "Flash" lost. He was so ready for the Qantas flight out of Bombay to Melbourne and most likely in a straitjacket.

Before a typhoon hit Southern India and marooned us in Bangalore for three days without hitting a ball, I had a classic doubles match. Another crowd-pleaser. On this occasion, my partner was a Mexican player, Emilio ("Pollo"), our first time together, a virginal duo. I seemed to have more doubles partners than Gunga Din. I was starting to get a complex about my doubles ability. Or, maybe everyone wanted to be my partner!

Our opponents this encounter were Chico Hagey (an affable Californian) and Paul McNamee, my fellow Aussie "Macca" and I were yet to have our infamous win over Vilas-Tiriac in Rome when they supposedly tanked to us. Now, this time "Macca" was going in the tank. He had already lost his singles, collected his around-the-world air ticket and was so out of there. We were informed of this intended tank before walking on court. Chico was cool with that, he was already California Dreamin', ready for home.

But "Macca" wanted his moment of fun before he left us poor buggers in India. In our five-minute pre-match warm up Macca requested a few up, some practice overheads, as we all do in the final preparation. He proceeded to purposely mishit every smash deep into the crowd. Shanks and sixes out of there all over the stadium. It was like a cricket match at New Delhi and the crowd were loving it. He must have hit 20 balls out of there with the occasional one somewhere in the court. The crowd would collectively sigh each time he missed.

Paul would look down at his racquet in bewilderment, then with an impish smile as he did it again. The match was very light hearted after that warm up. The tank job was perfect, very well executed and entertaining. Paul was as popular that day with the crowds as their great cricket star, Sachin Tendulkar, or even "Flash" Letcher the day before.

"Macca" was gone. But three days later so was my partner. He was tired of waiting around for the rains to subside. "Pollo" just split for Mexico City. He did leave a message at the hotel telling me he could not wait around any longer. Thanks mate. I did get some sweet comeback on my amigo a couple of years later. I beat him in the final of a satellite tournament in Halifax, Nova Scotia. He behaved very poorly in the match and was thrown out of the final Masters tournament, which followed Halifax. Justice.

We sat around our hotel during the three days of rain, bored silly. At this stage, no one had become ill in India. We had all heard the horror stories about the dreaded Bombay Belly. One of the Aussie Davis Cuppers had contracted something bad during his duty on the subcontinent against Pakistan. He carried this parasite in his belly for another six months or so.

One thing to make me a little nervous was the local beer, which came in rather big bottles. Very tasty, however, but we often noticed small insects trapped in the bottles. Were they not sterilised before filling? Maybe the alcohol killed the germs. We made sure to not drink any water and even brushed our teeth with Scotch whiskey. But it only took one slip up….

On the last day of the rain, when the sun reappeared, a bunch of the Aussies had a fun game of cricket on the hotel lawns. It was so British, a game of cricket and a spot of afternoon tea around four o'clock. The hotel staff served tea on the lawns and even brought out a nice cake for us. How splendid. But the cake was to be our downfall.

Everyone who played cricket that day became as sick as dogs. Bangalore Belly had struck that night. I thought I was going to lose my roommate, Chris Kachel. "Honker" had been diligent all week in his dental care, brushing in twelve year-old scotch whiskey, but now he was throwing up all through the night. The cake had done him in, poor bastard.

I came out a bit wobbly the next day and lost to Sashi Menon. He was obviously more experienced on dung even though a lot of his tennis was played on Californian hard courts. The Indians were tough on their own dung pile. My bout of dysentery hit me hard as I boarded the Qantas plane to Sydney. Maybe it was OK my doubles partner "Pollo" did leave town early, I could not have played the next match of doubles anyway.

I had survived my first visit to India. Barely.

The next year, the Indian Open was held in Bombay (now known as Mumbai). No one was sick this time. No cricket was played or cakes eaten.

Before going to Bombay, everyone, particularly the Indian press raved at how nice our hotel was in that city. The Taj Mahal Palace Hotel was rated as a five star hotel. And it was. What an extraordinary setting, the impressive building opposite the Grand

Monument at the gateway to India. Well, maybe it wasn't quite five stars. My first night at the Taj, I was awakened late in the night by a tremendous amount of banging, bumping and scratching on the walls of my room. Someone was trying to break into the room through the wall closet. I was a bit scared and had my trusty metal tennis racquet at the ready. Not to worry, it was not an intruder, but just a horde of rats. Big nasty looking rats.

When I realised I was not under a terrorist attack, I was fine. But sadly in 2008 there was a disastrous terrorist attack on the Taj Hotel, 166 people died and the hotel was torched. Next morning I noticed the rat trap under the bedside table and we saw a few rats scurrying around outside by the swimming pool. These guys were big, as big as cats. No worries, no one contracted the Black Plague, not even a sign of the Bombay Belly this trip.

Looking back on my trips to India, it was a good life experience to see how the other half does live. Maybe all the spoiled (and some rich) tennis players should visit the undeveloped countries and experience their world. Here we were travelling around the world, often staying in first class hotels and being treated like royalty. And getting paid to hit a few tennis balls. But seeing India and spending a little time there was a shock to the senses. To see this seething mass of humanity, and how they survived, particularly in those mega cities where we played tennis was sobering. There was an extraordinary amount of poverty, people sleeping on the sidewalks in makeshift cardboard shelters. And beggars by the hundreds, confronting you as soon as you walked out of the hotel doorway. More beggars rapping on the windows of our taxi as we waited at the traffic lights, some thrusting their deformed limbs through the windows clawing for a few coins. It was hard not to give something, however if you did dozens would overwhelm you in no time. The local people who had something like wealth or higher social standing seemed inured to this squalor around them.

They seemed so callous to the poor and the squalor in the streets, just turning a blind eye to it all.

I have not returned to India but I'm sure it has become modernised in the 21st century. And the conditions for the tourists are way better now than they were back in the 1970s. Just like China, they have come a long way.

In this country of one billion plus more people there is still abject poverty and horrible living conditions. 500 million people may own a mobile phone but another 500 million people don't have a toilet. Quite a statistic.

I think we came away from India with a new perspective on life. We were so lucky in our own countries. Somehow winning a tennis match was not that important, not a number one priority anymore.

Footnote: We lost our good friend and my sometime roommate Cliff Letcher in 2007. Known as "Flash" or "Rump" to his tennis buddies, Cliff succumbed to melanoma at his home on the Gold Coast in Australia. He was about to turn 55. His legacy is wonderful and I smile to myself when I recall some of his exploits on and off the tennis court.

Apart from the S.E. Asian circuit in the latter part of each year, I visited some more countries in Asia, this time in the early months of the year before the regular season started. In 1978, I spent roughly two months in five different countries in the role of tennis coach. The Department of Foreign Affairs in Canberra (our State Department) was looking for a couple of tennis pros to tour some neighbouring countries representing Australia as goodwill ambassadors. Our government thought tennis clinics and exhibitions was a nice way to woo these people and improve relations between Australia and the developing countries of Asia.

Canberra contacted our Davis Cup Captain, Neale Fraser, requesting two coaches to do this tour. Neale asked me and I jumped at the invitation. As my first wife Jenny was an international player also, he must have thought we would make a good team as husband/wife coaches. We were very green in the coaching business but were willing to give it a go. Also, I don't think the point of this whole exercise was to make tennis champions but to introduce some of the locals to the game and show them how it was played.

We set off with our diplomatic passports (for once, I did not have any issues with immigration officials) on our journey to Indonesia, Singapore, Philippines, and the more under-developed nations of Burma and Bangladesh. I was not keen to travel to those last two destinations mainly because the air travel seemed a bit suspect. But these two countries were ultra-keen to have some tennis coaching from abroad probably for the first time. Tennis was such a minor sport in Burma and Bangladesh particularly, so it seemed like good diplomacy to bring some tennis coaches from the number one tennis nation in the world (yes still number one in the 1970s). Interestingly, the tennis officials of these National Associations were people from the military, usually high ranking, and they were also people of power in their governments. I could see where the Department of Foreign Affairs was going with this mission.

Burma was a real revelation. Entering the capital Rangoon (now known as Yangon) was like turning the clock back to around 1945. I imagined things had hardly changed since British rule finished in 1947 not long after the Second World War came to an end. In the colonial quarter of Rangoon, the Edwardian buildings were in sad disrepair and very decrepit looking. There were no modern cars in the streets just lots of old American Jeeps, possibly leftover vehicles from the war days.

Our hotel, the iconic Strand Hotel, was where Rudyard Kipling spent his days writing those classics. Sadly this great hotel was past it. It was not in the best condition with rusty brown water in the bathrooms, frequent electricity brown-outs and general disrepair. And the hotel food was horrendous.

I wonder how Rudyard was inspired to write while living there?

We only lasted one night in the Strand Hotel and then were rescued by the Australian High Commissioner who housed us with the First Secretary in the Aussie compound. Now this was living. Food was flown in from Australia (even vegemite) and there was clean water and regular electricity supply. Life was good in the Aussie compound. The only thing we were warned about besides drinking the local water was to avoid the many rabid dogs roaming around. One bite from those puppies and you would require a dozen or more injections into the intestine. Did not sound like a lot of fun.

Tennis was real low key in Rangoon. We did some clinics and a couple of exhibitions involving the local players. I don't think they had seen any tennis here except for some exhibitions by the Americans during the Vietnam War days. Arthur Ashe and Stan Smith, the US stars, had toured Burma during their military service days.

We had another coaching stint organised up country in Mandalay, the place romanticised by Kipling. Again, I was not too keen on the domestic flights in this part of the world but we had no choice. Due to the insurgents (I'm not sure who was fighting who here), it was forbidden to travel by car or train. So, plane travel it had to be. I had bad feelings about this one.

I recall our early morning flight out of Rangoon on a propeller jet. We were delayed for some time on the tarmac, ostensibly due to fog, but maybe there was some security threat. We did make it to Mandalay with a stop in a little place called Pagan. I was a real white-knuckle flier in those days. Maybe it was the old reconditioned planes (did they service them at all?) or maybe it was the lack of airport security in that part of the world. But it was no fun. Anyway we survived the flight up to Mandalay and returned safely. We also survived the dust and heat of Mandalay. The tennis officials had sent a minder with us, like a KGB agent, on our trip.

I could not see the point of this escort because he was not a translator. Obviously, we had no Burmese speak whatsoever, and he had no English speak, so he probably was some kind of agent to make sure we weren't spies from Australia. After all, Burma was communist controlled with not many links to the Western world. One week later we were in the Philippines when we saw the news of a plane crash in Burma. "Plane explodes on take-off from Rangoon; all 55 on board killed" reported the Manila newspaper. The same 7:30 flight we had taken on the previous Monday morning, Rangoon to Mandalay, had been blown up minutes off the ground. The insurgents had put a bomb on the plane after all.

My fear of flying did not improve much after hearing that grim news.

It made me think about how safe air travel really was. Imagine how many plane trips all the world's tennis pros had taken over the years since air travel had become routine? There must have been thousands upon thousands throughout dozens and dozens of countries. The only player I can recall going down was the great Mexican champion, Rafael Osuna. He had died in a private plane crash over Mexico, nevertheless not on a commercial flight

One of our top Aussie players had a harrowing experience, a close call if you will in the mid 1970s. Dick Crealy ("Digger or "Creels") was en route to Johannesburg, South Africa for the men's doubles Masters late in the year. This tournament was for the best eight doubles teams who had accumulated the most points in the Grand Prix events throughout the year. "Creels" partner in Johannesburg was Tom Okker, the Flying Dutchman. Apparently the guys were rendezvousing in Nairobi, Kenya then catching the flight south to Johannesburg together.

"Creels" had flown in from Australia while Tom was catching the Lufthansa flight from its origin in Frankfurt. The flight stopped in Nairobi then continued on to South Africa. However, on arrival in Nairobi, "Creels" learned he did not have a confirmed seat on the connecting Lufthansa flight. Somehow, he had been bumped and there were no seats available. The plane was totally full out of Europe. "Creels" was a gentle soft-spoken big man but he could snap sometimes, go a little ape if you will. No amount of begging or threatening could get him a seat on the plane. He must have been devastated because this was the last and only flight that would get him to the tournament in Johannesburg on time. "Creels" was going to disappoint his doubles partner, Okker, and also lose a lot of prize money guaranteed to them just for showing up.

Totally frustrated, he repaired to the airport bar to have a few cocktails. Apparently he was still seething as he watched the Lufthansa jumbo plane take off from Nairobi without him. But to his horror the plane crashed shortly after take-off, an instant fireball. He must have been thinking of his poor partner as well as all those unfortunate souls on board (59 people died) It was a disaster. It was the first Jumbo 747 to crash in the plane's history.

By a twist of fate Okker somehow missed the connection to Frankfurt. He was coming from his home in Holland to Frankfurt. "Creels" did not know this at the time he was just thinking his friend had been killed before his eyes. He had fought the airline manager tooth and nail to have a seat on this hapless plane. Screw the tennis matches. They were both alive, that was more important than a few tennis games. Poor "Creels" must have been shaken to the core though.

Bangladesh was the one stop I was a little apprehensive about. Maybe it was the thought of those old Fokker planes out of Calcutta, Rangoon and into Dacca, the Capital. But in retrospect it was probably the most exciting stopover of the Asian cities. Bangladesh is one of the most populated countries in the world: 140 million or so in this small pocket of land about the size of Tasmania, on the Bay of Bengal. It is predominately Moslem. A very poor country, it had been hit by so many natural disasters over the years from disastrous floods to famine and disease.

Tennis was almost unheard of in Bangladesh. I think we were the first foreigners to do any coaching clinics in the country. Possibly by this fact, I was made a life member of the Bangladesh Lawn Tennis Association (Jenny was not included, after all this was a macho man's world). The big sport here was the world game, soccer. I don't know about their boxing skills but just before our visit, Muhammad Ali had visited Dacca and he was treated as a superstar there. Maybe because he had adopted Islam and also he was possibly the most recognised man on earth.

Again, like Rangoon, we were housed in the Australian High Commission compound. No tummy upsets and good Aussie food. It was sobering to see the terrible sights, the poor beggars being manipulated by pimps, and just the extraordinary poverty everywhere we turned. It was not uncommon to see a dead body lying in the street.

We had sneaked into Dacca between military coups, the forced Government takeovers. There was one not long before we arrived and another after we left the country. Seemed like this was a regular occurrence. Again, just like Burma, the military chiefs were the officials controlling the Tennis Federation. Our man in Dacca was Major General Ershad who was president of the Tennis Association. A few years later Ershad became President of Bangladesh in yet another military coup. I think he, too, was deposed in another coup a few years later.

Our last leg of the S.E. Asian tour was the Philippines. The first two stops, Jakarta and Singapore had not been particularly exciting but I found Burma and Bangladesh so interesting. Definitely off the beaten trail, these countries were not the typical tourist destinations.

In the Philippines we were guests of a retired Brigadier General and his family. The Filipinos are lovely people, ever friendly and happy. We were treated well and did some tennis clinics in Cebu City and the wonderful resort of Baguio in the mountains of northern Luzon. But there was very little organisation here. Grandiose plans and ideas but nothing ever eventuated it seemed. I was to learn later this was normal stuff in the Philippines.

We happened to be there during the Philippine National Championships. This is their closed tournament to determine domestic tennis rankings. I had no right to play but the General insisted I compete. Well, we were not doing anything constructive in the way of coaching, so maybe this was some goodwill in a way. We were back on the shell of Rizal stadium once again, but not as hot this time of year. I was starting to be a good shell player and won the tournament. So much for any diplomatic relations here, but I don't think the local players actually cared that much: they were ever smiling and happy, win or lose. The Filipinos are such fun people.

Jenny and I had an interesting and exciting two months in S.E. Asia. It was fun being a tennis player/diplomat. On our return to Australia, the Department, of Foreign Affairs, Canberra asked us to conduct another tour in east Africa. We jumped at the opportunity. Same thing, this time in Kenya, up in the highlands at Nairobi as well as down on the coast at Mombasa. A very fun time and a wonderful country to spend some time in. It hardly seemed like work to us. But soon it came time to return those diplomatic passports and head back to the regular tennis tour once more.

Chapter 8

American Journey

Another journey took me to the USA.
It took me a long time to get to the United States. I had played fairy exclusively in Europe for about five or six years yet I had not set foot or hit a tennis ball in the U.S.A. To be honest, I was a little apprehensive about going to the big league, a little over awed with the prospect of playing tennis on the big stage.

I did extensive tennis travelling all over Europe during those years. But unfortunately, I was to lose almost a whole year, 1973, due to injury and 1974 was sort of a recovery year trying to get back after the long layoff.

So in early 1975 I made my first visit to the United States.

Backing up a little to explain my debacle of 1973. Way back as a junior in High School at Toowoomba I had broken my collarbone, that all-important clavicle you sort of need in order to swing the tennis racquet. Normally I begged off the school tennis competition, which was a very low level of competition and I was usually in-volved in cricket or in more serious outside tennis tournaments. I was to play one meet on a cold winter's day. In the warm-up for my singles I hit an overhead smash and there was an audible crack. It hurt a bit. After sitting out the singles I went back for doubles. Sitting in the bench in the cold wind did not help much, obviously, and in the doubles game I experienced another loud cracking sound. It hurt a lot this time. Maybe it was a fractured collarbone? The old arm was immobilised but I somehow reached home on my bike. My Mum cut the shirt off and said I needed to get some medical attention. However, my Dad disagreed that my clavicle was broken (he should have known better, he had broken his a couple of times). Being the typical, tough country man and a former Light Horse soldier, he said "Son you can't be running off to the doctor every time you scratch yourself". Well, he was pretty right. Out in the bush where I grew up that was realistic: I had survived axe wounds, spider bites, etc. (no snake bites, luckily) without running off to the doctor.

My Mum fashioned a sling and off I went back to school and played in a tennis tournament a few weeks later, serving underhand. The clavicle did mend in time, but badly. Essentially the bone mended incorrectly and a big calcium deposit appeared. It would come back to haunt me later.

However there was some good news from this little injury. Five years after fracturing the collarbone, in 1972, my number came up for the National Army Service. This was like the lotto, your birthday was put in a barrel then some were randomly pulled out. Looked like I was a goner for 18 months with the prospect of service in Vietnam. I cruised through the medical test. However I decided to appeal my fitness because they had not seen my messy collarbone during the first medical.

Second time around the doctor said, "Sorry mate, I don't think you can fire a M1 rifle in that condition. Get outta here, you have a lifetime exemption from Army Duty". It sounded all right with me, a tour of the tennis circuit sounded much better than a tour of Vietnam but more importantly 18 months was a long time out of my tennis life.

In the latter part of 1972 during the early winter months I had played an Indoor series of tournaments, the Dewar Cup Circuit, throughout England, Scotland, and Wales. My arm was bothering me more and more and the injury was not helping my game or my confidence.

I had the bright idea of having surgery in England (free on the National health system for British Commonwealth subjects) then spending the winter in Europe recuperating. I would come out rejuvenated in 1973 ready for the spring season in April. Also my finances were very sad, so this manoeuvre would save me an air ticket to Australia and return. Sadly though I would miss the summer season down under but I definitely needed to fix my busted clavicle once and for all.

I had the surgery, a bone graft in fact, in London. The hospital was the Wimbledon and Merton, a few lobs from the All England Club. I had no clue regarding the recovery time and I don't think the orthopaedic surgeon had any clue either. Five months down the road after having my arm strapped to my chest 24/7 (like Lord Nelson) I finally received the OK to remove the sling. On asking him about rehab because I was so eager to get back to the tennis circuit once more, he said "Lad just go down to the pub and bend your elbow as often as you can with those heavy pint glasses" great advice, doc. Thanks mate.

During all these recovery months I worked in Harrods of Knightsbridge that very expensive department store (the world's biggest then) where Her Majesty the Queen of England shops once a year. I was a salesperson in the sports department. It wasn't easy wearing a suit and tie with one arm immobilised and doing everything left handed. Maybe I should have tried playing tennis as a lefty?

The most depressing part of all of this was sitting around incapacitated when Wimbledon rolled around in June. I had the surgery in February and I still had not hit a ball by June. And to add insult to injury this was the golden year to play Wimbledon. About 70 of the top men had supported an ATP boycott and pulled out of the singles. This was a great opportunity for a journeyman to get into the tournament proper and maybe do some damage. Except for the big names of Nastase, Kodes and a young Connors (he was to win next year in 1974) the tournament was up for grabs. John Newcombe, Stan Smith and many other star contenders would not be competing in the 1973 Wimbledon

My home that year was Mrs Drake's B&B in Putney. I was sulking in my room too depressed to even go out to Wimbledon to watch. Just taking the bus to work in Knightsbridge and missing the tennis like crazy. I could not even bear to watch the tennis on the BBC.

I did get back on the road again but not until the end of the summer on the Continent. I had one test run up at my old fun tournament, Felixstone in July. It was too early yet even though the surgery was done five months previously. Somehow I won the doubles with my friend from the USA, Armistead Neely, while serving underhand sometimes but my poor arm took a beating. It was so atrophied and weak. Back to London and a couple more months of rest. I was very disheartened.

A comical aside to my surgery happened a couple of years later in Ireland. I was playing in the Irish Open. Traditionally, this was a big tournament on the grass courts at the old Fitzwilliam club where lots of name players would come in preparation for Wimbledon. I had a good tournament winning the men's singles. The headline in the sports page next day in Dublin was "Aussie wins Irish Open. Played five years with a broken racket" I do believe the reporter and I were separated by a common language (to steal a phrase from his fellow Irishman, George Bernard Shaw). Wish it had been a broken racquet. A racquet is easier to mend than a broken collarbone I found out.

Prior to the A.T.P. being formed and the advent of the complicated rankings the American circuit was essentially one where you had to be invited. I'm sure there was some politics involved in who received the invite but you pretty much had to have a very respectable National ranking to get a foot in the door. This all changed when the men's Grand Prix and the ATP were formed and there was a true international circuit of major tournaments. From then all the acceptances were controlled by an unemotional, unbiased computer which held no favourites. You either had the computer points or you did not. The traditional U.S. circuit was mainly located on the east coast at exclusive clubs. Swanky places like the Longwood Cricket Club, Boston (where the American championships were held originally), the Newport Casino and Hall of Fame (Rhode Island), Merion Country Club (in Pennsylvania), South Orange Lawn (in Orange, New Jersey) and of course the private club of Forest Hills (in Queens, New York) site of the U.S. Championships. There were other old established tournaments but I never had the chance to play this circuit. Maybe my invitation was lost in the mail? All tournaments were played on grass on this East Coast circuit. Los Angeles was a fixture too but that was on hard courts out west (there is not much grass in California) at the Los Angeles Tennis Club.

In 1975 when I first visited the US in the early part of that year, there were some satellite tournaments starting up with computer points in the USA as well as in Europe. The ATP was two years old so things were starting to move.

These tournaments were for the fringe players who were trying to get some computer points to make it into the major league. It was not easy because there were hundreds of good players with the same goal and those points were as scarce as hen's teeth. Basically you had to play a five-week circuit of satellite stops and then the points were allocated to the top 16 guys in the overall finish. Not easy. Everyone was good and everyone was very hungry for points.

That first satellite circuit was held in Florida. It was started by a couple of nice guys who themselves were trying to break into the big time like everyone else. Larry Turville (whose Dad was actually the president of the USTA at the time) and his friend, Armistead Neely, started the inaugural W.A.T.C.H. circuit. WATCH stood for World Association of Tennis Professionals. A pretty ambitious-sounding moniker. I was to learn World was a generic word in the USA (like the World Series of baseball and the World Championships in the basketball NBA, both domestic competitions). You mean, there were other countries in the world besides America?

The first tournament on the Watch circuit was in a quaint little town called Vero Beach on the east coast of Florida. Vero Beach was known in America because the famous LA Dodgers spent their time there every year during spring training. Apart from that claim to fame Vero Beach was just orange groves. Smallville, USA but a nice little town.

This was where I made my assault on the American tennis scene. To get to Vero Beach from Brisbane, Australia was quite a trip as it turned out, and one of the longest journeys I have ever undertaken. It rivalled my epic trip from Hong Kong into China a few years later. Some of the Aussie players had found some cheap air tickets out of a travel agent in Melbourne. These were remarkably cheap tickets in fact. I had jumped at this deal because it saved a lot of bread. The only catch with these tickets was you could not change your air travel itinerary once the tickets were issued. It was not possible to re-write the ticket at a later date at some other travel agency or airline. No worries, we knew where we were going (sort of) so no need for changes.

Prior to setting off for the USA I had been invited to a couple of days playing exhibition matches in Manila, the Philippine capital. OK a bit out of the way but they guaranteed some good money to show up for the exhibitions. This was my first time flying on El Cheapo. However, on the eve of the flight up to the Philippines I received word the exhibitions had been cancelled. Wow, that sure did not sound like Filipino organisation. I sure became used to that kind of stuff over the coming years. Now the problem was with the air ticket which we could not re-write. Holy crap on my first El Cheapo flight! With no option I dutifully flew to Manila and spent the good part of a day waiting for the long haul flight to San Francisco on my journey to Florida. After that came a long wait at the airport in San Francisco in order to catch the red eye across to the other coast to Miami.

Guess I could have checked into a hotel for the day but I was very frugally watching the few dollars I had. My first taste of this awesome country was San Francisco airport and being continually harassed throughout the day by Hare Krishna groups and other religious people. Wow, this America was already shaping up to be a weird place going on first impressions.

On arrival in Miami next morning (what day was it anyway?) I found the small commuter plane up to Vero Beach was not departing that day at all. Plan B was to catch the Greyhound Bus up the coast. Now, those bus stations I found out, are quite disturbing places, too, anywhere in America. After waiting about six hours in Miami for my flight that did not happen, I took the interminable journey up the coast stopping at every little town along the way. Was I heading for Guangzhou again? I finally arrived around midnight amidst a tremendous downpour. Everything in Vero was shut down. Zero in Vero. No hotel or other accommodation available. Suffice to say I was a tad buggered, jet lagged and disorientated after 45 hours on the road through numerous time zones. I was scheduled for a tennis match sometime that morning. Welcome to America.

My first tournament experience turned out to be very enjoyable though. I ended up in great housing with the tournament director and his family. That was one nice thing about the American circuits, the extraordinary hospitality. It was so fun to stay in someone's home rather than in a bland old hotel room in downtown Anytown, USA. A lot of those city areas in America were not the most salubrious places to stay.

Another good thing about Vero Beach was my roommate, Cliff "Flash" Letcher. Cliff was not quite into his mooning phase yet, but he was always good value on and off the court. He actually had a great tournament and made it through to the finals on the har tru (American synthetic clay court) surface.

Although he lost to a South American human backboard he put up a good showing and was very entertaining for the crowds. "Flash" had nicked himself a few times while shaving that morning and the cuts had opened up during the final. Probably a result of the vigorous towelling down during the match in the Florida humidity. He looked like the Man from Borneo, this big, lumbering guy with blonde hair flowing, a blood streaked face and cursing like an Aussie trooper. The Americans loved him. This was his first trip to the USA also.

The Watch circuit took us all over Florida. Such a big State the Sunshine State .The weather is generally quite humid and windy and a little like my Queensland, the other Sunshine State. It seemed like the average age of the residents was about 100 but there were many pleasant towns especially along the coastlines. We played in places like Daytona Beach, Fort Myers, St. Petersburg, Longboat Key, and Tampa. Also, Orlando, Jacksonville and Tallahassee off the coastal track. A good first taste of the USA although I had only experienced one of the 50 States.

In subsequent summers I came back to play the US circuit in the bigger league. These tournaments were mainly in the northern States during July and August leading up to the US Open in early September. This was part of the Grand Prix Circuit so were always very strong events. But now that the ATP computer ranking system was in full force you could get into the tournaments with a half decent ranking (top 100 or so in the world).

During some of those summers I would play a few weeks after Wimbledon on the European Continent and then head to the States. There was the Swiss open (in Gstaad), the Swedish open (in Båstad) and the Austrian open (in Kitzbuhel), all in July. These are great tournaments in such wonderful resorts. Gstaad must be the most beautiful little town on the planet, a picture postcard village in the Swiss Alps.

The first US tournament of the summer was scheduled at Newport Casino, Rhode Island. This was always a fixture on the US circuit and Newport is an idyllic spot. The tournament is played at the International Hall of Fame courts on grass. It is the only remaining grass court event on the calendar in America to this day. In fact, there are only a handful of grass court events remaining on the world tour: the lead-up tournaments to Wimbledon at Queen's Club, London, Eastbourne and a couple on the Continent during the same time (Halle in Germany and another one in Holland), then Newport Rhode Island after Wimbledon. Grass is a dying court surface sad to say. What a wonderful quaint club, The Hall of Fame and Casino in the main part of Newport and walking distance to those extraordinary mansions on the cliffs looking out to the Atlantic. It's the site of the movie "The Great Gatsby".

It's funny how you remember places by won or lost (usually won) tennis matches. I have a knack of forgetting the losses—too many to remember anyway—and just recalling the wins. My last memory of Newport on the US tour was a doubles match in the loss column. My partner was a fellow Queenslander, the "Animal". Dale Collings was a big, kind of intimidating figure with long reddish, blond hair. Everyone on the tour knew him as "Animal" and I don't think anyone knew his first name, Dale. Even his mother called him "Animal", I believe. He had a fierce countenance, a perpetual scowl but he was really a docile animal, his bark was much worse than his bite.

In Newport our first round match was against the number one seeds, Stan Smith and Bob Lutz. They were a legendary team in those days, probably only bettered by John McEnroe and Peter Fleming, or as Fleming used to say "The best doubles team in the world was McEnroe with anybody".

"Animal" and I were a virginal team but we did well together. We went to a final set tie-breaker against Smith and Lutz. Up six points to three in the breaker, triple match points. "Animal" had two service points to close it out.

Now "Animal" had a monstrous serve. On the fast grass courts it was a lethal weapon. Only that year at Wimbledon he had served a zillion aces in his match with the Italian star, Adriano Panatta, losing in five sets. Panatta was so pissed off with this big red man in a yellow baseball cap acing him at will. Something like 50 aces for the five set match.

Shut the gate my friend. All "Animal" had to do was bomb in a big serve and then we shake hands, and say thanks for coming. Unfortunately that did not happen and we snatched defeat from the jaws of victory (I accept some fault for not poaching on one of the "matchies"). We lost 9-7 in the breaker. That really hurt. Needless to say, Smith and Lutz went on to win the tournament.

That signalled the end of the "Animal + Agro" team. Those matches where you have match points then lose the match seem to stick in the memory bank for a long time. A lot of scarring to the brain matter as well

I did return unexpectedly to Newport ten years or so later as a senior player. On this occasion I had fond memories winning the National Reebok 35s event, this time in singles. A better memory to savour and a wonderful presentation evening at the Marble House, one of those extraordinary mansions on the Bluffs formerly owned by the Vanderbilt family.

Apart from Newport on the grass, the other US summer tournaments were played on clay, the artificial greenish grey clay, which was known as "har tru." This was a medium to fast surface, much quicker than the terre battue of Europe. The US Open had been held at the private club of Forest Hills in Queens, New York. This was played on grass forever, just like two of the other Slams at Kooyong (Australia) and Wimbledon. Now moving into the mid

1970s, Forest Hills switched from grass to "har tru" in conjunction with the other Grand Prix stops on the summer circuit. In 1977, Guillermo Vilas won an extraordinary 53 consecutive matches on clay cumulating in his win on the dirt in the finals of Forest Hills.

Not long after the change from grass to clay the US open moved across Long Island to the National Tennis Centre at Flushing Meadows, site of the World Trade Fair in the 1960s. It was a public facility and the court surface was switched to hard courts (kind of a Plexi Cushion). Now all the summer tournaments went to hard courts rather than clay. Could you please make up your minds USTA .What's it going to be, grass, clay or hard courts?

Regular stops on the summer circuit were in cities like Washington (DC), Indianapolis (Indiana), Cincinnati (Ohio), Louisville (Kentucky), Columbus (Ohio), Atlanta (Georgia), all very hot and sweaty in July-August. The Washington tournament stood out as one of the hottest weeks. One day it reached the highest temperature of that year (107 °F). Earlier in that same year, in February, I had played in the Indoor tournament at Georgetown, Washington and it was the coldest day of the year (around freezing) and snowing a ton.

That summer stop in D.C., at Rock Creek Park, they provided oxygen on the side of the court for those players who had breathing problems in the severe humidity and pollution.

It did seem a little weird. Was this on court assistance? Was oxygen an illegal substance? This was a long time before random drug testing or the rule changes involving injury time outs and bathroom breaks.

A couple of the tournaments in New England were much more pleasant to play during the summer. Stratton Mountain (Vermont) and North Conway (New Hampshire) were two beautiful resorts where we played. Some cities had tournaments for a couple of years then they quit. Perhaps they did not make any money.

Boston, Chicago and Cleveland fell by the wayside for some reason or another.

There were two tournaments during the tournament year in America everyone wanted to play. One was the Island Holidays Classic out in Maui, Hawaii part of the west coast swing. The other one was in Las Vegas the Alan King Classic. Why Sin City? Maybe it was more for the shows and the gambling but every man and his dog wanted to play the King Classic at Caesar's Palace. Also Caesar's had a lot of money to throw around.

This must have been the only tournament in the world, apart from the Grand Slams, where the top ten players in the World rankings would be in the same field. Nowadays the top guys are mandatorily committed to the Masters Tour 1000 Series, nine tournaments on the next tier below the Slams. So you could get the top four players meeting each other quite frequently. Back in the 1970s, you would never see Borg and Connors showing up at the same tournament unless it was a Major, or unless it was in Las Vegas.

The host of the Vegas tournament was the well-known US comedian, Alan King. During the final, bikini clad girls would bring out money on court in wheelbarrows loaded full of silver dollars. First prize was $30,000, a lot of money back then. And a lot of silver coins.

One year in the 1970s (I can't recall the exact year) my former doubles partner from Toowoomba during my first years on tour, Ross Case, made it to the singles final. Ross must have beaten quite a few big names to get though. Everybody in the 32-man field was pretty much ranked in the top 32 in the world. Someone had to knock off Jimmy and Bjorn, after all.

I have forgotten who he knocked off on the way but in the final Ross lost an amazingly tight, great match to the monster serving American, Roscoe Tanner. It came down to a third set tie-breaker. In the pre match TV coverage, the announcers had introduced Ross "From the tennis capital of the World, Toowoomba, Australia" instead of "From Toowoomba, in the tennis capital of the World, Australia". We used that line for a while; it certainly put our little Toowoomba on the map. Now it is officially known as the Tennis Capital of the World. Wow. That is quite an accolade. When Alan King presented the trophies and cash to Roscoe and Ross, he said Caesars's was going to award $30,000 to each finalist. Equal prize money awarded to both players because of the high standard of the match. Ross hit the jackpot, an extra 15 grand for losing. That has never happened again in any other tournament in the world since. Equal prize money for the finalist. It could only happen in Las Vegas.

I did not have any success in that tournament or at the tables for that matter. In fact, my only time there, I did not qualify for the singles. No shame, only two guys qualified. But I did enjoy the great hospitality of Caesar's Palace and the craziness that is Las Vegas.

Another US circuit I played in the spring was the Southern Circuit. These were satellite events, smaller tournaments than the big league Grand Prix tournaments but each with individual ATP points. Of course, a lot of good players showed up for these events. They could smell the computer points from afar and they came out of the woodwork. I think you had to find satellites in Outer Mongolia, or somewhere more remote, if they existed, somewhere out of the way where players would not travel for points.

The Southern tournaments were in the Deep South towns like Shreveport (Louisiana), Birmingham (Alabama), Little Rock (Arkansas), Atlanta (Georgia) and Greenville (S. Carolina) to name a few. One I enjoyed was in Augusta, Georgia. Here I was in the Mecca of golf but I did not appreciate it. In those days I believed golf was just played by old men in funny trousers. I had no interest in the Masters at Augusta National even though it was golf's equivalent of Wimbledon. Nowadays I would give my left nut to see the Masters, or to be near it.

One year my housing was kind enough to invite me to an equally beautiful course, adjacent to Augusta National where my host was a member. I did hack it around, chopped up some azaleas and sliced into the dogwoods, but sadly golf was not my bag then.

In the Augusta tournament I was coming off quite a long lay-off due to my chronic back problem. However my ranking was healthier than my back and I was seeded number one. Lacking mobility and a lot of confidence I managed to lose first up to a young kid from Georgia. As it turned out this kid was sponsored by the singer, Kenny Rogers. Kenny lived in Athens, Georgia and was a fixture at the NCAA championships held there in his town every year. He was a real tennis aficionado. I never actually saw him hitting balls but he was an avid fan nevertheless. He also sponsored another player out in California and he would come to the matches at UCLA regularly to watch his protégés play.

In Augusta the word was Kenny was going to give this kid the chop after one year of sponsorship. He was not doing well, not getting any results. However, his win over me (a top 100 player) gave him a new lease and another year of monetary backing. Oddly I never saw the kid again on the tour. Maybe he became Kenny's roadie coach. I might have cost Mr Rogers a few more dollars in sponsorship but he probably had more wheelbarrows of silver dollars, I guess, just like Alan King had out in Vegas.

The third Grand Slam of the year was in New York City. The US Open. It was held in early September with the Labor Day weekend in the middle of the tournament. The end of summer but it was still quite hot and sweaty. Probably nice to play at night but those matches were the feature matches reserved for the stars.

The Open was the least favourite of the Slams for me. New York City was such an exciting city. But just getting from the hotel in Manhattan out to the courts at Flushing Meadows was an expedition. And when you made it to Flushing it was like, please let me play my match and get out of here. There was not the atmosphere you felt at Wimbledon or Paris. I really enjoyed walking around the courts at Wimbledon watching bits of matches or popping into the player's section of centre court or court one to catch a match in those intimate arenas. Maybe it had something to do with grass rather than concrete. At Flushing it seemed like a baseball game. Hot and noisy, jets from La Guardia airport roaring overhead, smoke from hamburger stands drifting across the courts. The atmosphere was like the baseball at nearby Shea Stadium, home of the N.Y. Mets rather than at a tennis match. Perhaps that is just New York. And Arthur Ashe stadium was just too big and impersonal. Seating for about 20,000 spectators and anywhere at the top seemed like miles away from the players down on the court. I think a corporate box was the way to go.

My first time to the Open the tournament was still played at Forest Hills Club in Queens. It was a quaint club, a bit different to the public courts across Long Island at Flushing. However I had to undergo the rigours of qualifying which was held at the Port Washington Tennis facility, a club with lots of" har tru "courts both inside and outside. That's the place where a young John McEnroe was learning his skills on the dirt. No wonder I had trouble with him on the dirt of Paris. In those early times there were six rounds of qualifying; three rounds of "pre-Qualies" for so called sub-humans (guys with a poor ranking) then three rounds of qualifying proper. I was in the sub-human class the first year but somehow I reached the final sixth round. For some unknown reason (maybe logistical) my last round went indoors. The main tournament was outside of course, but qualifiers had to play wherever they were ordered. I ended up losing a ball-tearer, 7-6 in the final set to a good local New Yorker. This was in the era of the original tie-breaker, the 9-pointer a real Russian roulette of a breaker. Imagine one point possibly deciding the whole thing at 4-4 in points? Match points for both players. I lost one of these, a heart breaker. But I'd been there before at Wimbledon a couple of times earlier on. Glory days. Or zippo.

My next time at Forest Hills I did a little better. No "Qualies" for me, thank goodness, my ATP ranking was high enough to get me into the draw proper. The surface was still clay (har tru) but it was about to go hard court when the venue changed to Flushing Meadow. Gee whiz, in a space of about four years the US Open had made the changes from grass to clay to hard. Imagine if Wimbledon suddenly decided to go to dirt courts or Paris switched from terre battue to grass overnight. Wouldn't that be sad?

I was bundled out in the second round. At least that was progress. I think bundled is a great term, better than just losing, the "L" word. The media forever have used bundled out, usually when they refer to one of the seeded players being ignominiously beaten in the first round. Often when these players get further in the draw they' bow out 'maybe going as far as the final before bowing out. I did have my share of bundling over the years. Never lost per se, just bundled out.

One of my favourite lines regarding losing came from my old compadre from Spanish days, the incomparable Greg "Blue" Braun. One year, in Kooyong during the Australian Open "Blue" had sneaked into the main draw through "Qualies" (an admirable feat) and was up against the legendary Ken Rosewall. The match was on centre court and nationally televised. The courtside presenter firstly introduced Rosewall with his mouth-watering accolades a mile long. Everyone knew "Muscles". Then the presenter said, "Greg, we have not seen you here before on centre court, can you tell the fans who you have beaten in your career". Blue who looked like he had just left his horse up in Biggendan, Queensland, responded in his inimitable drawl: "Well mate I can't tell you who I've beaten, but I've lost to every Tom, Dick and Harry"! Thank you, Greg. Priceless. He could have added Ken to the list an hour later. I could relate to Blue's comment. We have all lost to Toms and Harrys and I have definitely lost to some Dicks.

Well, that was the US Open. Not too many fond memories but New York City is a wonderful place, the centre of our universe. I think any town or city had special meaning if you did well there and you won some big matches.

One of my nice memories of New York was having lunch at Windows to the World the restaurant on the 107th floor, on top of the World Trade Centre. My friend who took me to lunch was employed in the South Tower as a financial planner with a big firm (I never found out if he survived 9/11).

I returned to New York a number of times in the 1990s when my playing days were done and I was living in California. My old buddy, Ron Homberg (one of America's top players, a former Davis Cup star and world ranked number seven) invited me there in the fall for a big annual charity event. Ron, a native New Yorker put together the tennis pro-am part of the charity event. The charity was for the Franciscan Sisters of The Poor a Catholic organization in the City. It was a great weekend. We had tennis, golf, running events and a monstrous charity dinner at our hotel in Times Square. Each year they invited a superstar celebrity athlete to honour at the dinner. I really enjoyed my short stay each year I went to New York, staying in Times Square and jogging in Central Park. So relaxing and no hassles like getting out to Flushing Meadows or trying to win a qualifying match.

I played a few tournaments on the west coast including the tournaments at Los Angeles and San Francisco (although I never made it to the Cow Palace) and of course, everyone's favourite in Maui.

Still in North America I did get to play a satellite circuit in Canada during one summer. We were chasing those invaluable computer points but in this case we had to chase a long way from Victoria Island, British Colombia, right across to Halifax, Nova Scotia on the Atlantic side. There were stops in Calgary, Toronto and Quebec City with the finals in Montreal. Canada is a big country and it seems even bigger when you drive across most of it. I did have a soft spot for Canada because I won the last two tournaments including the Masters and the overall circuit (all for those bloody points).

America was a wonderful country to play tennis in. The travel was easy between cities, just hop on a plane or drive those lovely interstate highways. The hospitality was great. People were always friendly, especially in the South. Everyone spoke English. What more could a travelling tennis pro ask for?

Little did I know then that America would become my home when my tennis travel days were over. It's where I would meet my beautiful wife and where my boys would be born.

Chapter 9
Journey into the Wilderness

When it is time to quit? I think every player knows when it's time to step away from competitive tennis. Even so, if you have a passion for the game you never really quit playing the game. But doing it for your livelihood is a little different. Pete Sampras had the ideal retirement: he won the US Open once again (title number five) then he hung up his racquets for good. No more. Not every player can do a Sampras, though.

By the end of 1980 I was near the finish line, my tennis-playing journey was almost over, but I was not quite ready to face the reality. Better to burn out than fade away, right? Early in 1981 I travelled to Auckland for the NZ Open. I did not know it then but this was to be my last singles match in a Grand Prix event, at least in the major leagues. The old body was not holding up too well with the chronic back injury recurring more and more frequently. My last match was a loss to the American Billy Martin. I think he was struggling with his fitness too. Not many years later Billy had a double hip replacement in his thirties. Quite extraordinary for a young man but he had done a lot of pounding on the hard courts of California. I don't know who was hurting more then in Auckland, Billy or me.

Thirty years of age is not too old to play tournament tennis. Though it does feel old when you are hurting in some way. Not many of the professionals last too long into their 30s these days. Back in another era guys like Gonzales and Rosewall played forever, as did Jimmy Connors, still performing at the highest level. Ken Rosewall was still going strong into his forties with some extraordinary performances. He was in the Wimbledon and US Open finals (losing both to a young Jimmy Connors) in 1974 just a few months short of his fortieth birthday. Rosewall was superbly fit of course and never seemed to have an injury. Or maybe if he did get hurt he would not tell anyone, just go and hide for a while then come back to competition only when he was 100% fit.

I wasn't as smart as Rosewall. Playing injured is really damaging to the psyche too. You are not going to win many matches anyway and then the confidence suffers. In retrospect I should have taken the time off the tour to rehab my back then jump back into the circuit recovered and eager to go again. It was somewhat of a catch 22 situation because I could not afford to take months out of the tour. I felt I had to keep grinding away and make some money while my ranking was half decent. The current pros have the injury protect ranking system now so their ranking will be frozen during the enforced time off. Yes, I should have sought some professional attention for my back injury and then done some rest and rebuilding in the gym. The year out of the game in 1973 with my collarbone reconstruction had made me a little impatient. I did not wish to go through that kind of lay off again. Hey, only two injuries (collar bone and lower back) in eleven years of competitive play, was not all that bad. But it's not so enjoyable when you are not winning many matches and getting poorer.

Still I wasn't done yet. In early 1981 I jumped off to S.E. Asia and played a couple of smaller tournaments in Singapore and Kuala Lumpur, Malaysia. Previously I had spent about two weeks in Singapore during the Dept. of Foreign Affairs tour in 1978. Here I discovered a place that rivalled Manila and Bangkok for sweatiness. The small island (with about three million inhabitants) is located around three degrees from the Equator and it seemed like the rains would come in over the ocean and dump on the island about three or four times a day. The temperatures may not have been higher than in the other S.E. Asian cities, but it was equally as humid. During one particular tournament in Singapore, the matches were scheduled for the late afternoon and evening under lights. Still we sweated and sweltered. Our shirts were so soaked after a few games we had to change them while our shoes and socks were totally saturated after a set. We changed out of our squelching tennis shoes because the court was getting wet and it was difficult to stand up. It was like we had walked in the nearby ocean in all of our gear. If you wanted to lose some weight this was a sure way to drop some pounds just in one match.

While in Singapore I met a Chinese businessman, Mr Teoh who was a real tennis enthusiast. Teoh suspected I was looking for an alternative to the tennis tour, something to phase me out from the tournament play. He proposed I hang out in Singapore and work with a handful of the promising young players. Ostensibly, Teoh was a shipping and mining magnate in the S.E. Asian area but he may have had some underground connections also. He could well afford to bankroll these coaching clinics. For some unknown reason he was persona non grata with the Singaporean Government and also was at loggerheads with the local tennis body, the Singapore Tennis Association. I could understand that because they appeared to be a very inept old-fashioned organisation. Albeit Singapore was a small country it was pretty sad they could not field a Davis Cup team to represent them in the Asian zone qualifying. All the surrounding Asian countries had Davis Cup representation, but not Singapore.

Apparently the Tennis Association did have some extra funds to use on coaching but somehow it was squandered. For example, during my stay there they spent a huge amount of money on one exhibition match with the superstar Bjorn Borg and the American Davis Cup star, Roscoe Tanner (runner up to Borg in the 1979

Wimbledon final). I felt this kind of spending did not help foster junior tennis one bit or help their status in the International scene. It actually helped fill Bjorn and Roscoe's pockets. Hey, someone like me could have better used that money over a long period of time to help with the National team and with junior programmes. Oh well, not to be. So Teoh and I did our coaching underground and independently from the SLTA. I really enjoyed my time working with the junior players. Our courts were in Changi Village a stone's throw from the notorious prisoner of war camp where the allies were interned in the Second World War. I was not as tough on the kids as the Japanese guards were on the prisoners but we worked hard in the hot, humid conditions everyday. It put them and myself in good shape and it proved a good time in improving my back condition.

After my little stint in Changi (not the prison) I decided to just wander off to Japan and play some challenge tournaments. The itch to compete was still there. These tournaments were like second tier events with good computer ranking points each week. But why was I doing this? Who cared about rankings or points if I was not going to use them again? My days of playing on the big stage in America and in Europe were over. In my mind, I knew I was done but it's pretty hard to just quit overnight then walk away from the game.

Yes, I was seriously drifting now. But maybe something would just appear for me to get into. Coaching perhaps? There appeared to be a lot of potential for tennis to develop in S.E. Asia. China was still a sleeping giant but soon it would awaken to this tennis game. My interest was more in S.E. Asia and it seemed these countries needed a kick in the butt to get their tennis into the modern era. I could see myself in the coaching role in one or more of these countries, there was definitely potential in the area. A couple of American organisations had targeted the hotel and resorts throughout the South East Asian region but no one was helping the National bodies get out of the doldrums. Tennis in these places was amateurish, like it was still stuck in 1950.

In the meantime I was off to Japan. A little different this time, not in Tokyo where I had been a regular for the Japan Open but this occasion it took me to cities like Kyoto, Nagoya, Chigasaki and Nishinomiya.

1982 rolled around and I saw a coaching job offered in our ATP weekly magazine. The position seemed exciting, advertising a pro job at a big club in Zurich, Switzerland. There was also the possibility of playing interclub matches, which was usually pretty lucrative. Some time back I had played a season in Germany in a small town near Stuttgart. The great Aussie player and fellow Queenslander, Ken Fletcher, had asked me to take over from him for a season. "Fletch" the infamous "wheeler dealer", gambler and entrepreneur was moving on to bigger ventures. The Germans were very serious about their inter-club tennis and threw great money at the big name players to play the Bundesliga. Even guys like Boris Becker and Ille Nastase were signed up for key matches in their respective clubs.

I knew the Swiss too were into their club tennis so I was looking forward to this opportunity and to start my coaching career. The only coaching I had done previously was during the Dept. of Foreign Affairs tour a few years earlier. So I put Asia on hold for the moment. Off to Europe for me

However after accepting the position and jumping on the plane to Zurich, I received a big kick in the guts. The organisation that was placing pros. in various European Clubs informed me on arrival in Zurich that the job had fallen through. Something they could have told me before I left Australia. However, they had a backup teaching job at a club in Germany

Crestfallen but still optimistic that things would work out, I went off to Bonn in search of this wonder job. After all, I had come a long way to Europe so I best make something work. The good news was I had some kind of coaching position, the bad news was it was in a very small club outside the capital Bonn without the possibility of playing in Bundesliga, Oberliga or any league level club matches. This was small potatoes, kleine kartofflen. A quaint town and a nice little club but with only a few indoor courts and a couple of outside courts. I would have been much better off in nearby Bonn or Cologne playing for some of the big well-known clubs. These clubs had teams in Bundesliga as well as the lesser division of Oberliga, and they paid well.

Oh well, guts it out I did. First thing was to learn German. My four years of high school French was not going to help here. Luckily for me, most of the younger students who took lessons in tennis had a great English understanding as English is mandatory from grade school in Germany. However for my older students it wasn't easy. Lots of sign language, some rudimentary German expressions and somehow I managed. My tennis terminology was pretty good. I think my favourite term was ausholen (backswing). I used it frequently, maybe often in the wrong context.

Looking back, my eight months in Germany contained some of the most depressing days in all my tennis travelling times. At least during my shoulder rehab days in London I had some friends to hang out with and everyone spoke English. Here I was in a foreign country, living in a tiny apartment, and not doing very well in my first coaching position, the so called new career. Where was I going with this venture? There was no future here and I was not even making any decent money for my efforts. The Germans are very organised people, a smart race, but not too friendly. Everything seemed so business like, cold and formal and they only let their guard down when they had a few alcoholic beverages. Only once during my time in Germany was I invited into a German home. I did feel truly like the gast arbeiter, truly a very foreign worker.

However I did escape a couple of times to play some tennis tournaments. One I enjoyed was in Berlin at the old Rot-Weiss Club. I had played a tournament here back in 1970. Berlin was fascinating, full of history from the war. I must have read every book on the military history of Germany in the Second World War so it was great to visit places like Spandau, the Brandenburg Gate and of course the Berlin Wall. During this visit another Aussie friend and I took a day trip through Checkpoint Charlie into East Berlin. What a contrast: the grey, drab lifeless streets in East Berlin compared to the bright lights, nice shops and restaurants of the Kurfurstendam, a wonderful boulevard in West Berlin. I was glad to have done the trip though Checkpoint Charlie. Who was to know in almost six years' time, it would not exist and the Wall would come down?

One memory I recalled from the 1970 Berlin tournament was my road trip from Berlin to Paris. I had bummed a ride with a Canadian player and his wife. They opted to drive through Germany on their way to the next tournament, the French championships. It turned out to be a fairly dull drive though the DDR, on the autobahn with lots of barbed wire perimeters and no getting off the autobahn for a drive through the countryside. I could understand why people never escaped from the West into East Germany it was only one-way traffic. We had one amusing incident though at the Berlin exit control. The border guards really gave our car a thorough going over, checking inside, out and underneath. For what, I don't know? However the Canadian girl had left a book on the front seat, one she was currently reading about the Krupp family. This was the family who had armed Germany during the war manufacturing the armaments for the Nazi war machine. They made everything right up to Big Bertha, the humungous gun named after Frau Bertha Krupp.

The guard who confiscated the book went off his nut, ranting and raving in German but to no avail. We had no clue why he was yelling at us. Didn't he know the war was over? The Red machine had overcome the Krupp machine. But border guards the world over have no sense of humour as I found out a couple of years earlier in Spain and also I was to find out one day in the future in the USA. Actually in retrospect, the East German guards might have been a bit nicer then the immigration guys at Los Angeles Airport.

I made my escape from East Berlin, East Germany and now from West Germany, after eight months of misery there. At least the weather was nice during my time in Germany and I did not experience any real cold and snow of a European winter. Yes, a good thing. It was time to get back to the drawing board. I left Europe and gravitated back to my old stomping ground, my second home, Singapore.

Singapore was just a marking time period. I had given up any possibility of working with the National Tennis body. They did not want to give up their antiquated ideas on tennis so consequently their best local players were going nowhere without hope of representing Singapore in Davis Cup. Because I was not welcome in this little clique I turned my attention to working with the expatriates in Singapore. There were hundreds of American and Europeans who were working on the Island mainly involved in oil and banking. I gave lessons and clinics to these foreigners at their very nice private clubs around the Island. Obviously I was not going anywhere with this but it was enjoyable and I was making some money while I thought about where else in S.E. Asia I could break in. Maybe the Philippines was calling?

Singapore was a good learning experience. It was like my home away from home and totalling my recurring visits there, I actually spent a year of my life in Singapore.

One of the very few tournaments held in the island nations was the Singapore Grass Court Champs. Each year they marked out some grass courts on one of the old British bastions, the quaint Singapore Cricket Club. It reminded me of the Wimbledon qualifying tournament at the Bank of England Club in Roehampton where they just marked out the grass courts on a soccer field. The Cricket Club,

147

right in the centre of Singapore city and in the shadow of the famous Raffles Hotel was a real throwback to the Colonial days when the British ruled. This quaint club surrounded by modern skyscrapers seemed so out of place in this bustling Chinese wonder city. One little piece of leftover colonialism, which I loved, was a sign of the entrance to the patron's bar at the Cricket Club: "No women or dogs permitted on veranda". I knew this was a chauvinistic world but you would think women could at least warrant their own sign.

The grass court tournament was often affected by the frequent rainstorms and the humidity was quite extraordinary. The competitors were mainly from S.E. Asian countries so it was not that strong an event. I won twice there and lost one final, each final against the Indonesian number one player, a wily and talented player but quite a crazy personality.

1983 found me at the drawing board once again. What now? Where's this journey going? I had gone up to Tokyo during the end of the Asian tour in 1982. My singles ranking was not on the radar but I did get to play doubles. It was mainly a commitment to my racquet sponsor Yonex that I had gone back to Japan. Then I finished off the year with a couple of tournaments in Bangkok.

While in Japan I was approached by a friend of mine, a Filipino player, with a proposal for me to work with the Philippine Davis Cup team in the capacity of National coach. My buddy, Beeyong Sison, was the best player out of the Philippines and he had good success internationally as a specialist doubles player. Beeyong explained his frustration with the National Tennis Association in his country and it was similar territory to what I had been through in Singapore. He was tired of the ineptness of the PHILTA, their grandiose plans and the inability to make anything work. Now Beeyong was going it alone with a little help from a few friends in very high places in Manila. One friend was the president of the Philippine National Bank (PNB), an avid tennis fan who was prepared to sponsor something new on the local tennis scene. The

PNB had previously sponsored the international tournament in Manila The plan was to form a new Davis Cup team, adding me as their coach then travel to Europe for all the big tournaments besides Davis Cup competition. Obviously the focus was on the Asian Davis Cup zone and an attempt to successfully win the Eastern Zone qualifying. Traditionally, the best countries in the region were Japan and India but now Beeyong wanted his country to get into the picture for the first time.

The team was comprised of two very good young players from Manila plus Beeyong, the seasoned older dog and doubles specialist, and an American import, Walter Redondo. We also had two very promising young Filipino juniors. Walter was a Californian with Filipino parents so he was eligible to represent the Philippines due to his ancestry (besides, he had not played Davis Cup for the United States which would have ruled him out). Walter was such a good player but almost a wasted talent. He had an extraordinary junior record growing up in California, better than anybody including Jimmy Connors, which is impressive to say the least. But Walter was not hungry like Jimmy. He looked like the perfect tennis player, textbook strokes, beautiful form, but he was not a grinder. Walter would have been a successful male model. Here was this handsome dude with the wonderful tennis game. But looking good did not count much in winning tennis matches. You had to get dirty out there even if it meant winning ugly. Sometimes you had to scrap it out.

Our new look team convened in Manila in early 1983. We were all excited about Davis Cup and the potential of this team. Our home base was in Quezon City on the edge on Manila and we trained at the beautiful Manila Polo Club in the heart of Makati in downtown Manila. At the Polo Club, one of the former top players of the Philippines, Willie Hernandez, ran his Tennis Academy for promising young kids. Willie was also employed in the armed services and had connections all the way up to President Marcos.

He was backing our team as far as helping with the training and was finding some money for us as well.

The future looked good for the team. We were surrounded by influential people in the Government and we had the backing of the Philippine National Bank. That was huge for us. Our team looked promising.

Suddenly stuff hit the fan. I was very aware that in this part of the world, corruption and graft were just the way of government and business. Terrible timing, but our main man, our sponsor, the president of the PNB was caught with his hand in the till. He had been siphoning funds away in some Swiss bank for many years and then happened to get caught right in the middle of our little venture. What timing. Why did he have to get busted now? There went our sponsorship right out the window. He was not going to help us much from jail. It's a shame he didn't give us access to his secret Swiss bank account number either.

After our plans were torpedoed we had to try Plan B. The new plan was to raise sufficient funds to get our way to Europe by conducting various exhibition matches and coaching clinics throughout the Islands. That sounded like a good idea; after all there are 7,000 islands in the Philippines. Surely, we could rake together a few pesos here and there, enough to get us going.

Over the next six months we did all kinds of exhibitions and clinics in every little place, no matter how remote. We went to Clark Air Force base in Angeles City and to Olongapo, Subic Bay, home of the US 7th fleet. We went as far north as possible in Luzon to Baguio, a beautiful resort, south to Cebu City and on to Dumaguete, and even farther south to Oriental Negros (Tuguegaro), such a remote and pretty place. Here they had probably never seen a foreigner with blue eyes and brown hair (it was still brown in 1983). I was a hit with hundreds of young kids at the makeshift tennis court. Some most likely, had never seen this strange game called tennis let alone a white man with blue eyes before.

Even though we eventually did not get enough bread together, we had a lot of fun in the islands. The Filipinos are such wonderful people, so happy and fun loving, always ready for a sing-along and a good time.

Our home base in Quezon City was at a villa owned by Beeyong's uncle. This uncle was once of the founding fathers of the Philippine Constitution. But at this time he was exiled to the USA, ousted by President Marcos. His friend "Ninoy" Aquino was also ousted by the Marcos regime and was living in exile too. Later that year, 1983, "Ninoy" was pardoned and make his triumphant return to the Philippines only to be assassinated as he stepped off the plane in Manila.

In Quezon City we had the run of the villa in a gated compound. I lived there with Walter, Beeyong and his cousin. When not doing our exhibition stuff in the outer islands and places, we trained at the Manila Polo Club. It was a nightmarish commute through the terribly polluted streets, a million jeeps spewing diesel fumes, with lots of crazy drivers and constant traffic jams. It made Bangkok traffic look like a pleasant Sunday drive.

Manila was still a violent place in certain parts. It had gone through martial law during the 1960s when every man and his dog carried a gun. We found out some people still carried guns. Beeyong's cousin had a buddy called Sammy who used to hang out at the villa, usually smoking weed most of the day. One morning, Easter Sunday, a couple of bad dudes came to our front security gates looking for Sammy. They were obviously not happy, maybe over non-payment for Sammy's candies. They made their way in when the maid answered the gate intercom. They saw Sammy fleeing down the driveway and both opened up with .45s as he fled. One big bullet tore through Sammy's butt and went straight through him. No one else was hit in the hail of gunfire and the maids were not hit thankfully. Sammy survived—a .45 slug can do a lot of damage—he lost a lot of blood and had a very sore bum for a while.

My sojourn in the Philippines came to a fizzling end. I should have known things would not work after my previous experiences there in Manila. But this was a different adventure and it could have come to something with a bit of luck. There was lots of chaos and confusion in the Islands. Tennis was just a gentleman's game, too nice. The locals loved the cockfights (which I went to once or twice) and boxing as well was very popular. I guess the locals enjoyed games of mayhem with plenty of gambling. Perhaps tennis was too placid a game for the Filipinos. Sadly our little team with big ambitions disbanded. We all went off in different directions.

My friend Beeyong emigrated to Switzerland and pursued club tennis and coaching in Basle. What a contrast to the Philippines, totally organised Switzerland. Pity he did not see his dream come to fruition with a great home Davis Cup team. However he did get to work with a promising lad in Basle, a youngster who would do wonders later on: Roger Federer.

Walter returned to Southern California. I think he should have gone to Las Vegas, he could have been a star there.

As for me, back to my second home, Singapore. Where else?

I felt like General MacArthur when I left the Philippines this time. I loved it there, but while the General had vowed "I shall return" I said, "I shall not return".

Return I did ,though, to Singapore. My work in Singapore was much the same as my last stay there. I was doing clinics with the expatriates at various clubs around the Island. Sometimes I did some gigs elsewhere. One was a trip to Brunei and another was an excursion to Balikpappan, also on the island of Borneo (Kalimantan to the locals). This deal involved doing tennis clinics for the Americans and Australians working for the US oil giant UNOCAL. Balikpappan is a restricted area in the southern part of the island but not really in the jungles of Borneo. Quite civilised, in fact. Another side trip from Singapore was to Bali, the beautiful island resort in nearby Indonesia. I took a group of expatriates from Singapore. We had tennis clinics in the mornings before the heat, then shopping and generally taking it easy at a wonderful family-run hotel.

One thing I did do in Bali was to experience the magic mushrooms, those hallucinogenic puppies famous in Bali. I did not know much about magic mushrooms and I had never experimented with any drugs, whatsoever. Guess I was a little naïve and my good friends who owned the hotel where we stayed encouraged me to try them once before I left the Island. Oh well, what the heck, it seemed like a lot of fun. The first few hours were extremely funny, very weird and wonderful. But the last part of this trip was extremely dark and frightening. That night was long. I wanted out badly but that did not happen till next morning. I felt like I'd had a near death experience, been to the dark side and returned. It shook me up for a while and was to change my view and my whole life perspective afterwards.

Later my Indonesian friends confided there might have been some LSD in the mushrooms as well. Something they could have told me previously! Also, one of the guys present during our little magic cheesecake dessert that night confided he had done this a lot out in the neighbouring island of Sumatra. One day the local villagers found him lying out in the field, apparently comatose, quite cold and clammy. Thinking he was dead they decided to bury him. He woke up when they were throwing dirt into the shallow grave they had dug! Wow, something else they could have told me before that evening. I definitely would not have experimented.

I went straight home to Australia after this last trip to Bali. I was a little shaken and very glad to be alive. Except for a quick trip to Singapore the following year to defend my Singapore grass court title, I said farewell to S.E. Asia. I was going back home to the old country, my Asian journey was done, or so I thought.

Chapter 10
Back Home

1984 saw me back in Australia. I landed a job as head tennis pro. at a large resort in my home State of Queensland. Kooralbyn Valley Resort was a beautiful place right in the middle of nowhere. Well, it wasn't far from Brisbane about 1½ hours drive to the southwest and a similar distance inland from the Gold Coast. Not far by Aussie standards although it seemed like in BFE (Bloody F..ing Egypt).

Koorabyn resort was wonderful, albeit isolated, with a magnificent golf course and a huge tennis centre. It matched the great resorts you see in the USA and the Caribbean. Maybe a little ahead of its time for Australia but it was an ideal getaway place.

There was not a lot of action in the tennis centre. However, once a month the resort would offer a Grand Slam tennis week for the tourists mainly travelling north to Queensland from the southern States. These Grand Slam excursions were each hosted by a former Grand Slam champion. No, that was not me, unfortunately. I would assist the three champions, Geoff Masters (The 1977 Wimbledon doubles champion), Mark Edmondston (the 1976 Australian Open Champion) and Wendy Turnbull (a multi doubles Slam champion, including Wimbledon). Geoff Masters' camps turned out to be the most patronised. "Eddo" was not as popular maybe because of his fierce looking personna. Actually he was quite friendly off the court, not as grumpy as he appeared in TV matches. Perhaps wrestling camps might have suited his personality better. Golf, the heart and soul of the resort, boasted one of the legendary golfers in Australian golf history, Mr Norman Von Nida. The "Von" was one of our great champions back in the 1940s and 1950s and was arguably one of the best teaching professionals in the world. Still teaching at age 70 in Kooralbyn. Apparently even the greatest golfers of the century, Jack Nicklaus and Gary Player, another legend from South Africa, would visit the "Von" in Australia for some swing advice. So he must have been good. Sadly I did not have any desire to play golf then. It was still the game for old men in my mind. One day, I recall, during lunch at the club "Von" said to me "Listen son, anytime you want to come out on the course let me know and I'll give you some free lessons". I replied "Sorry, Mr Von Nida. Thank you, but I'll pass this time". I did not have the heart to tell him my thoughts on golf. Here I was living in a villa on a magnificent golf course, time on my hands and an offer to be taught by one of the game's true legends. What an idiot. I'm kicking myself now for not taking him up on the offer.

Also, for a time, Kooralbyn contracted Greg Norman as their touring pro. Wow, this was a great environment for tennis and golf. It was really inspirational for those people visiting there.

During my stay in Kooralbyn Valley my passion was running. Always I had dreamed about running a marathon. This was the perfect opportunity. I had a one-year contract as the tennis professional at the resort and there was a lot of down time between Grand Slam weeks. Obviously I wasn't out on the golf course each morning. I hit the two-lane road leading out to the highway. Kooralbyn owned 50 square miles of land so there were definitely a few places to run. It was very peaceful out there, just me, a few 'roos and the open road.

I had read about Australia's great runners of the past, especially the legends, Herb Elliot, Ron Clarke and John Landy. Their guru was Percy Cerutty, a Harry Hopman-esque figure who drove these guys to greatness. Just like Hoppy did with his tennis stars. These runners lived in a Spartan camp amongst the sand hills of

Portsea, near Melbourne. They ate like rabbits (vegetarian) and ran like goats up the sand hills all day. No wonder they were almost unbeatable at the Olympics. In fact Elliot never lost at his distance, the mile, in his career.

As a teenager I idolised our great runners. Their training methods were so simple and basic, as was their diet and even their running barefoot. Maybe they learned from the natives of Kenya and Ethiopia. The only thing Percy had not foreseen was altitude training and it turned out to be Ron Clarke's downfall at those first Olympics held at altitude in Mexico City. Clarke was the world record holder at these distances but the altitude affected him. I must have fantasized more often about running into the Olympic stadium leading the marathon than I fantasized of holding the Wimbledon singles trophy aloft.

I did not do any sand hills in Kooralbyn Valley, just roads. However I was vegetarian like those running greats. So after about six months of pounding the roads I completed my first marathon, at age 33. It was a very rewarding experience and my time of three hours ten minutes was respectable for a rookie (not quite up to the three hours required to qualify for Boston and other big races). Maybe my barefoot days in the bush running around and playing tennis barefoot had built up the strength in the feet and legs. And I had no injuries before, during and after the marathon. I had proven my sports physiotherapist wrong. He had advised me not to attempt the marathon with my back condition injured during the touring days. He said I'd never make a marathon with my old back, the shape it was in.

So my hermit-like year in the Valley came to an end. It was not entirely fruitless. I achieved my marathon goal, played a little tennis along the way and my golf game stayed about the same (that is, non-existent).

It was also a soul-searching time, that year in Kooralbyn. I found out where I wanted to be spiritually and where I wanted to be physically. I had been drifting around for some time now, to Europe, in and out of Asia, and now Australia. It was time for the big league. America was calling. There was still that itch to keep moving. Maybe my future days were destined for the USA.

The tennis journey was not over, yet. I still had some travel, some wanderlust left in my body.

Chapter 11

America Beckons

The only difficulty I had in getting to the States was the job thing. I did not have one. Or any prospects on the horizon. Minor details. Hopefully something would come up. And something did come up, not too far down the track. My old (well, former) doubles partner and buddy, Ross Case, was back home in Toowoomba that Christmas visiting his family when we got together. Ross mentioned there was a position coming up at a wonderful Country club where he worked in Newport Beach, California. It was just a matter of getting my butt over to the States in a couple of weeks and the job was mine. He stressed it was only a minor coaching position at this swanky Country Club but it was a place to get my foot in the door then possibly later I'd find something more permanent in the Los Angeles area after some settling in time. No time to worry about a work visa—that would come back to bite me some years later—I packed a suitcase and left for the Promised Land.

A lot of the Aussie players went to the States after their playing days were done. For those who were keen to coach tennis this was the Mecca. Many guys ended up in the big tennis States of Florida and Texas and quite a few ended up in sunny California. The lifestyle in California was so similar to that of Australia.

After the tennis boom in the US during the 1970s tennis was still very healthy in the 1980s in California. There were lots of beautiful tennis clubs in the States. Tennis was never going to surpass golf but it was still quite healthy. The stars of the 1970s,

Jimmy Connors, Stan Smith, Arthur Ashe, John McEnroe, and Chris Evert in the girl's league, had done a lot to boost the sport but there were more superstars coming along in the 1980s. Players like Sampras, Agassi, Courier and Chang doing big things on the world stage. Tennis was going to be around a while and tennis pros were needed to keep the momentum going.

Newport Beach is a perfect location in Southern California, only about 45 minutes drive south of Los Angeles. It had been a playground for the Hollywood folks for a long time and Newport's most famous resident was John Wayne. His name added lots of glamour to the area and the Duke even had his own tennis club, The John Wayne Tennis Club, in the heart of Newport. It is such an affluent city and a perfect location for the sailing fraternity with its beautiful harbour. There are some seriously wonderful homes around the harbour and it's beaches. An example of wealth in Newport Beach is a couple of tiny islands in Newport Harbour and the only residents of the islands are two billionaires, each with his own little haven. Not a bad town to hang out in.

I had done about a month of R and R in Newport Beach back towards the end of my playing days in America. A number of the Aussie pros. had based themselves here in their playing days then ended up settling down in Newport, après touring days. Rod Laver was one of the first to settle here and then came Roy Emerson. They were then first and second with the most Grand Slam singles titles in history. Afterwards, incoming Aussies were Phil Dent, Ross Case, Syd Ball and others. I think Rod spread the word that this place was all right, perfect climate, a perfect playground and only about 1½ hours drive if you wanted to escape to the mountains for skiing and a similar distance to the desert wonderland of Palm Springs. The desert valley boasts around 300 golf courses, which makes it an amazing spot.

Ross Case and Rod Laver had played World Team Tennis in the late 1970s for the Los Angeles Strings (in the Laker's home, The

Forum) as well as for the San Diego Friars. These were only short drives from Newport Beach.

So I rolled up to Newport Beach and worked for about six months at the amazingly exclusive and beautiful Big Canyon Country Club (BCCC). Tennis was not a big part of the Country Club but at least I had a coaching position and I was in America. This was a good place to start.

The golf course was exquisite and difficult (Tiger Woods is an honorary member). I only played gold twice at Big Canyon and hacked it up quite royally. On my second time there I had sneaked behind a big oak tree for a desperate pee only to be reported by an irate resident. On making the turn at the clubhouse, the Club manager came out, stopped my golf cart and said "Mr Gardiner we have a major problem". I immediately thought there must have been a death in the family, or war had broken out in America. The manager said he didn't know what to do because the golf course resident was so embarrassed particularly for her out of town guests. Wow, here I was being so discreet up against a tree unbeknownst to me that people were perving. I apologised profusely to the manager and said something like "Shoot me at dawn".I never did play Big Canyon golf course again.

As usual I never gave much thought to those little details like work visas, green card, etc. I had showed up in the States on a tourist visa and simply commenced working as a tennis coach. The manager of the country club was a foreigner himself and he was not overly concerned about my status. After all they employed a number of Mexican workers at the club on a cash basis. These guys could have been illegal aliens or legal residents but no one asked if they had a permanent residency (green card), the genuine card or a homemade one. All I had was a social security card (obtained in the 1970s through my US manager) but that was no much help because it was stamped "Not Valid for Employment".

I was pretty naïve about immigration issues and the penalties for breaking the rules. I did not think about this paperwork much or at all. Looking back now, I had been through that little scare while entering or attempting to enter Spain in the early 1970s. Then later on in Europe in the 1980s I had ignored the registration (Anmeldung) to work in Germany for longer than three months.

For all their strictness to rules and regulations the Germans had not questioned me about my papers and did not send me off to Stalag Luft III.

In Asia the Singaporeans were almost as strict as the Germans in their model Island State. I had overstayed my 30-day tourist visa on multiple occasions. A couple of times I could not extend my stay further through the correct channels so I simply walked across the causeway into Malaysia at Johor Bahru, and then walked back into Singapore. Just like the Japanese invaders of 1940, through the back door. I did not worry at the time but Singapore immigration could have kicked me out. Singapore was extremely tough on any indiscretions: any involvement with drugs was a capital offence and even long hair was frowned upon. As a longhaired tourist entering Singapore you had a choice of a free haircut at Changi airport or you did not enter the country. So visa violations could have been a genuine issue. In the Philippines I worked for six months. We must have fixed that with a bribe in the right place. We did have some connections high up in the government so a little bribery would take care of the issue. It never did come up, this question of a work visa.

After my six month settling in period at the BCCC I moved up to the Los Angeles area from Newport, Beach. LA County was to be my home for the next two years. I did some coaching at the Brentwood Country Club for a time but mainly worked on private courts. One of my courts was adjacent to O.J. Simpson's home in Brentwood. I don't think O.J. was a tennis player, he was more a wannabe golfer and a member of the iconic Riviera Country Club just a three iron down the road in Brentwood.

I had a good tennis practice buddy from Ethiopia. His name is Gebrezedek Gebrezebehar, known more simply as Gebre, thank goodness. Gebre was a refugee from Ethiopia and somehow ended up as a teaching pro, appearing to coach every celebrity in Beverly Hills. We would practice at his tennis workplace the home of the famous actor and tennis enthusiast, Charlton Heston. "Chuck" Heston loved to hit balls with us even though his knees were shot from an aircraft carrier accident during the war or maybe from riding those chariots in "Ben Hur". Mr Heston had photos of all the great Aussie players on his little tennis clubhouse wall, including Laver, Rosewall and Emerson but oddly enough no photos appeared of American players. "Chuck" definitely had a soft spot for the Aussies (and Ethiopians).

Gebre was a lovely person. Amazingly this refugee from Ethiopia was now working with lots of celebrities in Beverly Hills. He had been introduced to America through his mentor the great Ecuadorian champion, Pancho Segura. "Segoo" and his son, Spencer, a successful lawyer in the Hollywood area had really adopted this kid into their inner circle. Gebre worked with many Hollywood people introduced to him by the Seguras. He did well, it's a big step from Addis Ababa to Beverly Hills but he made it in the big league.

Other private courts where I played were at the homes of Dean Martin and Diana Ross. Dean Martin's son, "Dino" or Dean-Paul as he preferred to be known was an avid tennis player and had aspirations to make it on the pro tour. I had played him a couple of times on the Australian tour and we played on some similar tournaments in Florida and in Central America. "Dino" joined the air force after his tennis days and acting days were done. Tragically, he was killed in a fighter jet crash when he was stationed at March Air Force base just east of LA.

Around this time in the mid 1980s I was playing in some Open tournaments in the LA and Orange county areas. Now I had reached the grand old age of 35 I was eligible for senior tournaments as well, or the beginning of the geriatric tour if you like. In Australia they refer to these old players as Veterans but I think I preferred Senior instead of Veteran. Veteran sounded too much like a war veteran. Maybe I had been through some wars, travelling around the world for the past 15 years fighting on various battle grounds/tennis arenas.

The competitive juices were still flowing. I had not played much since I finished up on the regular tour except for the odd foray into S.E. Asia, Germany and back in Australia. My old back was holding up OK and I felt as fit as a Mallee bull (apparently they are quite strong can and go all day) in the mating season.

California is such a strong tennis State. The players are good at junior level and are good at the senior level as well. Must be the nice weather all year round and plenty of competition right through the ranks.

I had some good success in the oldies league. It felt nice to win again. It had been a long time between drinks. It seemed to go way back to my junior tennis days. Perhaps competing for trophies and medals rather than prize money took some pressure off but there is nothing like winning to give you a boost. Even if it's winning the Ulan Bataar Open in Outer Mongolia there is nothing like a "W" to help the confidence. It felt good again.

I wanted to get onto a Senior Tour if such a thing existed. I was to learn there was a mini Senior Tour but only for the elite or household names. It was a fairly closed shop and you had to be a marquee player to get invited. Meanwhile I travelled to the US Nationals. These were the USTA sanctioned events for all seniors from 35 up to 85. There were four events in each age group throughout the States on four different surfaces: hard court, grass, clay and indoors (usually carpet). It is quite a good test of the player to tee it up on all court conditions. The winners of each event through all the divisions would receive a gold ball in an engraved box presented by the USTA. Hey, gold was as good as money, right?

My first National Championship was in Tuscon, Arizona. I couldn't believe how many "old" guys were coming out of the woodwork to play these things. Players I had known from the regular tour and a host of other hopefuls. I did well in my first tournament beating a couple of the favoured guys on the way to the final. But I fell at the final hurdle losing to a fellow rookie. My mistake was not to drink sufficient fluid out there in the desert and I almost did not make it through the match due to severe dehydration. Dumb and Dumber. You would think at 35 I would have learned something about playing conditions. Oh well, I settled for the silver ball, not the gold. A pity because the last match should have been my easiest one.

I skipped the National Indoors than went back east to South Orange, New Jersey for the grass courts and then played the clay in Tampa, Florida. My first gold ball came in Orange on the grass. Pity I blew the final in Tuscon because that would have given me the number one ranking for the year in the USTA. As it turned out I was ranked number two first year out as an oldie.

There was hardly any money in the seniors' events. Obviously we were doing it for competitive fun; one never seems to lose those competitive juices. A shame those miniature gold balls were not solid gold (just gold plated) otherwise we could have cashed them in at a pawn shop and made some real money.

One tournament I played in my first season did have a little prize money. The shoe company, Reebok, sponsored the National Teaching Pro classic with the final tournament at the Hall of Fame grass courts in Newport, Rhode Island. There were four regional qualifying tournaments throughout the USA with the four regional winners going to Newport for the play-offs. I had squeaked through the California section barely and then I won the round robin in Rhode Island. The winner received $5000, which was not a huge check by any means but a little more than those gold plated or silver plated balls. It was also good to go out on a "W" note at Newport. I had competed in the regular tour tournaments there a few times after Wimbledon without much success and also had lost that heart breaker doubles match with the "Animal" on my last visit to Newport.

Why didn't tennis have a senior tour like the golf tour? Well they did have a small, exclusive tour mainly for the superstars of the game, McEnroe, Connors and a handful of other marquee names. Perhaps a dozen guys in total. But this was a very small, elite bunch who were invited to play the tour and almost all these guys had a Grand Slam singles or doubles title in their résumés. Why did the golf tour have a successful senior tour, later called the Champions Tour, for anyone who was 50+ and could still stand up, while tennis had bugger all? I realised golf is a unique sport in that golfers can still play great golf in later years (50 and over) However tennis quality seems to fade away when players get a bit older. The nature of the two games is so different. Tennis is obviously more physical than golf. Jack Nicklaus won his 6th green jacket at Augusta when he was an "old" man of 46. Perhaps golf remains a better spectator sport than tennis when the players age a bit. Imagine someone winning Wimbledon at age 46? Not even Rosewall could do that. In golf there didn't appear to be much of a gap between the regular pros. and the senior pros. Whereas with tennis, being a bit more physical, the level drops off quite a lot due to the age factor. Of course there were the exceptional players like Rosewall, Connors and McEnroe who played at a high level into their 40s.

I should have chosen golf as my sport. Those guys had another crack at it when they turned 50. Here they were playing 30 or 40 weeks a year and still earning good money in their second time around. Admittedly many were financially secure from their younger tour days but they still had a chance to do something they still loved and were rewarded well if they were successful. Also it gave the average "Joe Senior golfer" a crack at the tour if he was good enough. At least he had a chance to qualify and follow that dream. The poor old senior tennis player did not have much to dream about. There was no tour, per se. He was just chasing little gold balls around.

My second year in the senior's was a little better than my first year. I finished the year number one in the USTA and only had one loss in the big four, that being in the clay courts down in Florida. There I lost to Charlie Owens from Alabama, not a bad loss. Charlie was probably one of the most under rated players in America on the regular tour and arguably their best clay courter in the modern era. He was also one of the most entertaining players of the time, too. Charlie was an under achiever who was happiest at home kicking back in Tuscaloosa, Alabama, a good old boy, rather than grinding it out on the tour.

That second year I competed in the I.T.F. (International Tennis Federation) World Championships. Fortunately for me, it was held in Southern California so I did not have to travel far from my new home. I was lucky enough to win the over 35 singles (beating a Hungarian guy who I knew from the regular tour). Great that it was played on hard courts because I don't think I would have won on slow European clay against the Europeans. So I ended up getting ranked number one in the ITF world rankings in 1987 and number one in the USTA over 35 rankings the same year. Not bad when I was happy enough to be simply the best player on my block.

It was now time to get a little serious about my visa situation. I had been in the States for a couple of years at this stage, working illegally if you will, just cruising on my tourist visa. I had winged it pretty well and paid my taxes to date but one never knew when the INS men were going to knock on the door. And the real threat of immigration issues could arise when I made trips in an out of America, usually at Christmas time to Australia

Luckily one of my tennis students and a good friend offered some help. Shelly Greenberg owned a prosperous ceiling fan company in Beverly Hills and an avid tennis fan himself, he decided to manufacture his own tennis racquet brand. This was produced in the same Asian factory where his fans were made. Shelly started the Stolle-Emerson Tennis (S.E.T.) Company with a little help using the names of our two Aussie greats. I played with the racquet in all my senior competitions and Shelly added me to the staff, I guess in an advisory capacity, so I was employed by SET tennis in a sense. Technically I was an employee of an American company. So off he sent me to his immigration lawyer in Beverly Hills in an attempt to procure the all-important work visa.

Mr Fraade had a swank office on Wilshire Boulevard but thanks to Shelly it wasn't going to cost me too many shekels for his time. The lawyer said he had obtained work visas for numerous famous rock stars from Great Britain, mainly, as well as their band members. The pictures and proof were all over his office walls. I am not sure why he was going in this direction rather than getting me the visa as one of the employees of Beverly Hills Fan Co.? I was not quite a famous rock star so Mr Fraade wasn't quite sure which approach to use with an athlete. He had never handled a work visa case for a non-entertainer before. That did no make me too confident because I was a long way from being a rock star.

He said why don't we go the famous tennis player route? My reply was that I was only famous in my own mind. Fraade reasoned my current number one ranking in the USA seniors and my current number one ITF World ranking would definitely carry some weight. OK, let's give it a shot. The only other obvious route to legality would be to find a cute American girl and marry her and secure a precious green card. Well, unfortunately, I had not met that cute US girl yet. My future wife, Danielle, was still a few years in the future so marriage was not an option yet (in reality she was still in grade school at this time. Cute yes, but a tad young to get married).

After a few weeks the immigration people came back with a rejection. Sorry mate, famous to them was somebody who had won the US Open or a Wimbledon title. This seemed like a weird criteria. After all they had no actual case records to go on. Oh well, Mr Fraade gave it a try. He said he would appeal the decision, nevertheless.

Then, weeks later very surprisingly, the visa was granted. The appeal had worked. Hallelujah. I was famous after all. This was case history, the first tennis player to get a work visa though this process. The next time I went back to Mr Fraade's office I was up there on the office wall with Rod Stewart and all his other British rockers. Je suis a rock star.

Armed with my new visa, which was valid for three years, I returned to the Newport Beach area where I had started my US adventure. This turned out to be home for the next 18 years. I bought a place, a condominium, not on one of the billionaires islands but not too far from the Newport Beach Tennis Club (NBTC), a beautiful club which would be my work place for quite some time. NBTC is a wonderful club with 19 courts, a great stadium centre court and a 25 metre swimming pool. Built in the 1960s, the club boasted Rod Laver as their original touring pro. Rod was a long-time resident of Newport Beach and this was his practice club when he was home, away from the tour. Fellow Queenslander, Roy Emerson, the Blackbutt Basher, lived in Newport Beach also and practised with Rod at the club.

In my time at NBTC our teaching staff owned some pretty impressive credentials. We had my fellow Aussies, Phil Dent and Syd Ball, both Australian Davis Cup members, Bernie Mitton, a South African Davis Cup star and a former highly ranked World player. Our touring pro. at this time, was the Australian Davis

Cup captain-to-be, John Fitzgerald. "Fitzy" was an eight-time Grand Slam winner in doubles including the Wimbledon doubles title twice.

One crazy morning at the club all the tennis pros. could have been eliminated from the draw so to speak when a light plane crashed onto the courts. Apparently the plane, taking off from nearby John Wayne Airport en route to Canada, lost an engine and the pilot was frantically looking for an emergency landing field. All four teaching pros' courts were lined up in the path of the descending plane. Sadly there was no way the pilot was realistically going to set down on a tennis court and he crashed onto Bernie Mitton's court. It exploded in a fireball. Nobody on the small plane survived the crash. Bernie was in the middle of giving a lesson to two club members, a man and his wife. Miraculously no one on the ground was killed. First reports were Bernie did not make it but as it was learned later, he was OK, obviously very shocked and shaken but otherwise uninjured. The plane had struck the fence just behind the baseline from where Bernie was feeding balls to his students. I noticed all the balls and Bernie's gear on the bench were burned. Meanwhile the other pros, including myself, were diving for cover on the adjacent courts as we saw the plane in trouble. I never did see Bernie's students again. I think they switched from tennis to lawn bowls, which was a little less hazardous perhaps.

I continued playing tournaments mainly at the senior level but with a few Open ones thrown in. I had to mix it up with the younger dudes occasionally.

My second year in the Nationals, I was ranked number one in the US over 35s. Each year there was an International team competition for over 35s called the Italia Cup and this year it was held in Mainz, Germany. The United States Tennis Association (USTA) invited me to play on the American team even though I was not a US citizen. I would have loved to represent Australia but they turned down my offer because I was not a resident of my home country. What irony. Our three-man US team consisted of one American (Charlie Owens), one Aussie (myself), and a Brazilian (Joaquin Rasgado) who lived in in Florida. Oh well, it would have been fun to play on the Australian team although this was not the Davis Cup by any stretch. I had never made the Aussie Davis Cup team, unfortunately, but I was a member of the junior Davis Cup team as a teen. That was also under the legendary Harry Hopman.

It was nice to visit Europe again especially returning to Germany where I had taught tennis in 1983. Our quasi-American team did well on the slow terre battue courts of Mainz. We were fortunate to have Charlie Owens on our team as he was arguably the best senior player in the world on dirt. Sadly we lost in the finals to the host nation. I lost to the number one German who was undefeated so far in Europe in the over 35 competition while Charlie pulled his hamstring when winning against their number two. Pity it didn't rain like it normally does in Germany because we could have knocked them off easily on fast carpet indoors.

It was fun to be on the team even though it was as a Yankee. And I enjoyed Germany more this time around.

Life was pretty nice in Newport Beach. I was teaching tennis at a fairly cool tennis club, staying out of trouble working and enjoying playing tennis tournaments. I had a chance to play golf, my new passion ,astoundidly, once or twice each week. And also being single was fine. Then Danielle came along. Danielle was an outstanding athlete who played tennis for her high school team as well as swimming for the school during the off-season. We met on the tennis courts and the rest is history. She went to college at San Luis Obispo on the central Californian coast on a five year tennis scholarship and then she came back to see me again.

We were engaged on Danielle's 24th birthday and were married six months later. There is a bit of a gulf in our ages but we did not care (her folks did though). Our wedding was in Hawaii on the beautiful island of Kauai. One of my good friends and a tennis buddy for 20 years, Steve Hunt, owns a wonderful resort on the Island. Steve and his wife, Janine, share their time between their home in Hermosa Beach, California and this idyllic spot in Kauai, called Kilauea Estates. They generously gave us the run of their romantic resort for our honeymoon.

We were married on the beach in Hanalei Bay in Princeville and it was perfect. About 50 or 60 family and friends made the trip to Hawaii from California and Australia. It was such a wonderful time and we've vowed to return to Kauai every ten years to do it again.

I was starting my run a bit late but soon I was a father for the first time. Our first son, Tyler came along the next year in 2004. He was born in Newport Beach and life changed a tad after that. Things became a little busier with both of us coaching tennis and doing the baby stuff.

Our next child, Luke, was born literally two years later also in the same Newport Beach hospital. We had our perfect little family. Yes, life was busy with both of us teaching tennis and juggling kids, but it was surely wonderful and new to me. We were lucky to have Danielle's Mum, Celeste, living about 20 minutes drive north of us in Los Alamitos. She was a great help, plus we had a Mexican nanny who cared for the boys when we were working.

Then things were turned upside down.

We had travelled to Australia around Christmas 2007 to visit my Mum in Toowoomba and to look up the other family members as well. On returning to California we passed through Los Angeles Airport (LAX) that wonderful chaotic airport. It was always with a little trepidation that I returned to the States after a trip away each time knowing full well I had overstayed my visa. By this time my work visa that Mr Fraade had kindly conjured for me had expired and now I was winging it once more on the trusty tourist visa. The tourist visa is usually good for 90 days (of course work was strictly verboten) and then one had to leave the country. I had survived about ten years on my tourist visa. The real danger was in leaving the USA and then re-entering. The Homeland Security people were going to ask questions why I had overstayed the maximum tourist time. Miraculously I had made about ten or twelve trips in and out of the States during these years mainly to Australia as well as a couple of trips to the Caribbean and one to Europe, all without incident. This also included a few trips to Australia post 9/11 when security was totally beefed up. This time at LAX with my little family in tow, I nervously went through the US channel at immigration control. The passport official asked me to step aside. My heart sank. The official told Danielle to go through to the baggage claim with our boys (then aged 1½ and 3½) but I was not going any place just yet. As it eventuated that was the last time I would see them for almost a year. Busted. Things were only going to get worse from here on in.

After lots of interrogation and threats by those badass Homeland Security officials I was locked in a room with two other detainees. I knew things were not good when the horrid female officer said, "Mr Gardiner you will not be entering the United States today and perhaps ever again. I feel sorry for your family".

I was in deep doo doo and I was already missing my family. About twelve hours later I was released from my "cell" and escorted to a Qantas plane by two burly, armed guards. Officially stated, I was "denied entry" which sounds a bit better than "deported". The Qantas flight was heading back to Brisbane where we had departed that morning. The airline staff had orders not to serve the prisoner any alcohol during the flight and I could retrieve my passport from the Qantas purser on arrival in Brisbane. Actually, the Qantas staff were very nice to me, the felon, during that heart wrenching flight in the wrong direction.

So I ended one of the roughest days of my life. I had not been allowed a phone call to Danielle who was now back at our Newport Beach home wondering what was going to happen. I was sick for her and the boys. Did they know I was on a plane back to Australia? Was I ever going to get back to America?

Well, those immigration people just can't take a joke. Really. So much for their security, when I could spend 21 years in California, the majority of that time without the correct papers. And I make a dozen or so trips in and out of the country without one question of my status. The irony of it all was there were most likely five million illegal immigrants in the LA area from south of the border. However they were probably smarter than me in not tempting fate by crossing back and forth across the border. Well at least I paid my taxes to the Internal Revenue Service during those years. That could have really upset some people and jeopardized any chance of getting back to the States again. The IRS did not care about my immigration status, obviously, they just said, "Show me the money" each year. But paying my taxes I figured was going to help my cause in returning one day to my family in America.

Yes that was a sad day in LA. I read a survey later that ranked LAX the number one most intimidating airport in the world when it came to contact with immigration and security people on arrival. I'll vouch for that. In my tennis playing days and later on in my travels I had slipped through the Spanish border control through the Pyrénées Mountains in the back door, walked across the causeway from Johor Bahru, Malaysia, into Singapore without incident and done the same walk across to Mexico at Tijuana, then straight back into the USA. But this time, they caught up with me in the land of the Free.

The obvious question is why I did not apply for a permanent residency, a green card, my entitlement after Danielle and I were married in 2003. Well I had already been in the States about 17 years by this time, most of those years illegally, so my request for a green card would probably have been denied. I was happy with the status quo and I did not want to make any waves at the immigration office where the line was about three years long anyway. There did not appear to be any haste in obtaining residency, or so I thought. Also, that would probably entail leaving the US and applying for the visa and residency from outside, in Australia. The only danger, meanwhile, appeared to be any travel in and out of America.

Gee, I had landed in a bit of a pickle to say the least. How was this going to pan out? Was this the end of my journey, a one-way trip to Australia? It appeared I was down a service break in the fifth and final set. Could I find a way to win this match?

The Department of Homeland Security people said I would not be entering the United States on this day or maybe ever again. This was serious stuff. I later learned this offence for visa violation carried an automatic ten-year ban. No entry to the USA through normal channels. Any visa request would be denied during that time period.

It was a traumatic time. I arrived back in Brisbane the next morning and then up to my old home, Toowoomba. My only possessions were the jeans and T-shirt I was wearing. My luggage was with Danielle in Newport Beach. My poor wife and young boys. When would I see them again?

Danielle called an Orange County lawyer immediately to get some much needed advice. He estimated I would get back to the States on a waiver visa in about six months because I had American family. His estimate proved to be a little off the mark, well, let's say totally off the mark.

I felt six months was tough, but acceptable. After all, I had broken the immigration rules consistently for some years. But ten years in exile was unacceptable to me, way too severe a punishment. We received some better advice later on when things were going nowhere. Our new lawyer, Juan, a very nice Spanish man spelled things out a little more realistically. He suggested I apply for a spousal visa waiver that would permit me to return to the USA. This spousal visa would allow me to re-enter the country

174

then immediately apply for permanent residency. In other words, I could go to the head of the queue for the Green Card. And this line was mighty long in California, about three years long before the wheels started turning.

It was a good plan but this kind of bureaucracy is painfully slow. I made multiple trips to the nearest US Consulate in Sydney. I had paperwork up to my eyeballs. And these people were treating me like a common criminal. I was not a terrorist. I just wanted to be re-united with my little family. That Department of Homeland Security was out to torture me, I believed. Their office for the Asia/Pacific region was located in Bangkok, Thailand. The US Consulate estimated Bangkok might not even look at my case for six months or so, due to the backlog of cases. What were these guys doing up there in Bangkok? Smoking dope? You would think the Sydney Consulate or the US Embassy in Canberra would handle the Australian cases.

I had to obtain all kinds of background checks to satisfy Homeland Security. Perhaps after all, I was really a secret agent or even a terrorist posing as a tennis pro. They needed a FBI check from Washington D.C. and a comprehensive medical check in case I had some contagious diseases I might take into America on my return. Another "snafu" was my fingerprints. I had the electronic prints done at the Sydney Consulate on my first trip there. Unfortunately these prints did not register due to my fingertips having little or no print remaining. Could I have worn it off from hitting thousands of tennis balls and golf balls? Was I a drug cartel criminal who had his prints surgically removed? I was required to return to Sydney for a simple inkpad finger printing. This was a one-minute exercise, which the local police station in Toowoomba could have done in a jiffy saving me a daylong trip to Sydney. You must be joking me now.

Another hold-up came from Bangkok. About one month after filing my reams of paperwork through the Consulate, they said

I had failed to dot an "i" on page 31 of my case file. Back to the drawing board and a one-month set back. After eleven months of this nightmare Danielle had had enough and decided to pack up and come out to Australia, to good old Toowoomba with our boys. It was too tough on her living in Newport Beach, working long hours on the tennis court, managing bills, and taking care of two little guys without her husband who was 7000 miles away in exile. With help from her family she put our belongings in storage and then leased out the condo and took off down under. Good for her, she is a gutsy girl.

Chapter 12

End of the Journey

In a way I could not believe I was back home in Toowoomba. It happened so suddenly. Was this really my home now? A bit of a shock to the system, one moment I'm living the good life in Newport Beach, the next moment exiled to Toowoomba, the so called Tennis Capital of the World. We had discussed the possibility that someday in the future we may move back to OZ. Was it a better environment in which to raise kids or was California still the dreamland? We had not envisioned this kick in the butt from US Immigration.

Eventually we were granted the spousal visa, my right of passage back to the USA. It took about two years of stuffing around with lots of extraordinary paperwork/B.S. Was this similar to the system in the former Soviet Union or in North Korea? Unbelievable stuff. Ironically, now, we were not going to utilize it. We said, "Thank you, but no thanks". Shove it Department of Homeland Security. California is wonderful but we are going to live in the carbon copy country, Australia. Besides, Australia has Medicare. Also we were blessed with the arrival of our little angel, Haven, born in Toowoomba General Hospital. Life is good again

It was nice to be home. I had just moved to the States when my Dad became sick and eventually died from bowel cancer. In 1988 I came home to watch him go. That was a difficult time. One positive aspect of my return to Toowoomba was I had a chance to spend quality time with my aging Mum. Back in 2005 Danielle and I along with our then one-year old boy, Tyler, had surprised Mum on her 80th birthday. We flew in from California and showed up at her favourite restaurant in Toowoomba. Only my brother Phil and his wife Judy were the ones in the know of our surprise visit. We certainly surprised those 50 or so family and friends when we walked into the restaurant. It was one of those precious memories to savour. We returned to Los Angeles and I went through LAX in a breeze. No worries that time.

I had come full circle since setting off from Toowoomba in 1969 as an 18-year old wannabe ready to conquer the tennis world. Over those twelve years on tour I hit tennis balls in 65 countries on six Continents. Somehow I never did get my invitation to play the seventh Continent, Antarctica. In the early years on tour we would write letters to the various tournaments hoping for a favourable reply, an invitation to come play the event. I guess I did not write to Antarctica back then. Anyway travel to the bottom of the world was difficult as well (A possible response from the tournament director could have been along these lines: We can offer you full hospitality plus accommodation at the Mawson Research Station, Antarctica. And $US100 guarantee. Court surface: outdoor ice.)

In my travel days, the 1970s, the tennis circuit was so very different. Back then the so-called circuit was a hodgepodge of tournaments scattered around the world. These were thrown in around the four majors. Nowadays the tour is a highly organized series of tournaments, a true circuit with a myriad of multi-tiered events in numerous countries. A lot of credit for this structure goes to the A.T.P. (Association of Tennis Professionals), the men's tennis body, which was formed in 1973. Without the A.T.P. we would not have had the prize money to grow so rapidly and it has probably increased 50 fold since those days. And the computerized ranking system changed the method of acceptance into tournaments completely. No more letter writing like in those years prior to the A.T.P.

Those four majors, the Grand Slams, grew into magnificent events. The Aussie Open, the final Slam of the year in the 1960s and 1970s, evolved from a somewhat parochial tourney into a veritable Grand Slam event. Now it's the first major of the year and every player, man or woman, in the top 128 in the world shows up to Melbourne Park. Of course the two million dollars first prize gets a lot of their attention.

I have no regrets over my twelve years out there on the road. In retrospect I would not have done things much differently. To travel with a coach/manager would have been a nice luxury. However we could not really afford an entourage, just getting ourselves around the world week to week for seven months at a time was tough enough financially. The new professionals can surely afford to employ some help on the road. Besides a coach and/or hitting partners (the women's tour mainly), some travel with a baby sitter, a nanny, or a physical therapist in their team. One top ten player currently travels with a sushi chef/nutritionist in tow. For me, I could have definitely used a psychiatrist in my camp on many an occasion.

A number of young hopefuls starting out on tour probably dream of winning Wimbledon or becoming the World's number one player. Lofty goals but you have to dream, right? I did not get there, for sure, but just competing at Wimbledon (eight times in either singles or doubles) was great. And, sadly, my best A.T.P. world ranking was only number 75 in singles, a tad short of the mark. (my best senior ranking was number one in the world in over 35s, though).

I am so glad I took a gamble and had a crack at the tennis circus. You only have one shot at it then your playing days are over, you are old, decrepit and done. One doesn't realize it at the time, but looking back at those years, the window of youth is brief and over in no time. Retired is for a long time. Thank goodness I did not listen to my maths teacher, Mr Grunke, in my senior year in school. Otherwise I could have been stuck in a chemistry lab or in some boring job instead of travelling the world. Well, boring maybe compared to being a professional sportsman, I think.

What a way to explore the world through tennis. It was a wonderful journey even though the valleys outnumbered the peaks, quite dramatically. That is sports. And that is the game of life.

Now, my journey was over. The journeyman had come home.

The End.

Lightning Source UK Ltd.
Milton Keynes UK
UKOW06f1823271217
315163UK00010B/406/P